W9-BWJ-873

Praise for *The Score That Matters*

"*The Score That Matters* is profoundly helpful, yet simple and accessible. And I really like the way Ryan and Brook use their different voices to make it compelling. This book is transformational."

—Patrick Lencioni, Author, *The Five Dysfunctions of a Team*
and *The Six Types of Working Genius*

"*The Score That Matters* is not just a book but a heartfelt guide to redefining success and finding genuine fulfillment. As a friend of the authors, I've seen firsthand the authenticity and wisdom they bring to the table. In a world fixated on external accomplishments, Ryan Hawk and Brook Cupps remind us that the real score that matters is the one that aligns with our purpose and values, guiding us on a path to becoming better individuals and leaders. This book is a beacon of light in a world often overshadowed by superficial accomplishments, and I'm grateful for the wisdom it imparts."

—Buzz Williams, Head Men's Basketball Coach, Texas A&M University

"People spend far too much time obsessing about external scoreboards and not nearly enough time thinking about their internal one. Hawk and Cupps offer an important corrective, arguing the most important measure is whether or not you are living in alignment with your core values."

—Brad Stulberg, Author, *Master of Change* and *The Practice of Groundedness*

"This book will not leave you alone once you've finished reading it. The questions and exercises that follow each contextually anchored chapter nag at you. It will make you itch to be a better human."

—Sherri Coale, Author, *Rooted to Rise*, and Hall of Fame Coach,
University of Oklahoma Women's Basketball

"Brook Cupps and Ryan Hawk have united to blend their individual talents and life experiences into one spectacular book on how to live a life of impact and fulfillment. Their intimate and personal stories will push you to new levels of leadership and solidify your learnings with actionable exercises at the end of every chapter. No matter your stage in life, this book will teach you how to 'Surrender the Outcome' in your 'Pursuit of Excellence.'"

—Rob Kimbel, CEO, Kimbel Mechanical Systems

"Ryan Hawk and Brook Cupps will make you rethink how you live your life. *The Score That Matters* is packed with invaluable strategies for achieving what you want *and* helping others along the way. It is a must-read if you care to live an excellent life."

—Vanessa Van Edwards, *Wall Street Journal*
Bestselling Author, *Captivate* and *Cues*

The

SCORE

That *Matters*

Also by Ryan Hawk
Welcome to Management
The Pursuit of Excellence

Also by Brook Cupps
Surrender the Outcome

The
SCORE
That *Matters*

GROWING EXCELLENCE IN
YOURSELF AND THOSE YOU LEAD

RYAN HAWK AND BROOK CUPPS

Matt Holt Books
An Imprint of BenBella Books, Inc.
Dallas, TX

Matt Holt is an imprint of BenBella Books, Inc.
10440 N. Central Expressway, Suite 800
Dallas, TX 75231
benbellabooks.com
Send feedback to feedback@benbellabooks.com

BenBella and *Matt Holt* are federally registered trademarks.

Printed in the United States of America
10 9 8 7 6 5 4 3 2 1

Library of Congress Control Number: 2023042835
ISBN 9781637745236 (hardcover)
ISBN 9781637745243 (electronic)

Copyediting by Lydia Choi
Proofreading by Marissa Wold Uhrina and Cape Cod Compositors, Inc.
Indexing by Amy Murphy
Text design and composition by PerfecType, Nashville, TN
Cover design by Faceout Studio, Tim Green
Cover images © Shutterstock / GoodStudio (tally marks)
    and © Shutterstock / pixssa (circles)
Printed by Lake Book Manufacturing

Special discounts for bulk sales are available. Please contact bulkorders@benbellabooks.com.

RYAN HAWK
*To Mom and Pistol: the ultimate example of
living by the score that matters most.*

BROOK CUPPS
*To the Christ-centered leaders who serve from a
foundation that is the North Star for all leadership,
leaders who recognize how flawed and insufficient they are
and surrender to the greatness God created them with,
leaders who ground themselves and their message
in the truth of Christ, not the truth of man,
leaders who understand that the only path to your
authentic self is through the love of God;
you are the leaders who know the score that matters.*

Authors' Note

This book was written by Ryan Hawk and Brook Cupps as a team. However, there are portions that are personal and written from a singular perspective. Those sections have been marked with the initials **RH** and **BC**.

Contents

Let's Gooooo!

If they weren't standing and cheering, the fans at University of Dayton Arena were sitting on the edge of their seats. The 2021 Ohio Boys Basketball State Championship was in its final moments as the lead seesawed back and forth. But those of us on Centerville High School's side were watching more than a game. We were witnessing a decade-long quest for excellence reaching its zenith.

BROOK CUPPS (BC): Years before, Centerville basketball decided not to focus on specific achievements or accolades. Instead, we chose to strive for excellence in everything we did, work hard to grow consistently, and trust our process to drive performance to the limits of our potential. In effect, we had surrendered the outcome of this daily quest for achievement. But as the seconds dwindled, that process was now in question. Would this process we had committed to be able to deliver our school's first state championship?

With 2:35 remaining in the fourth quarter, we were finally able to create a little breathing room. A perfectly executed pick-and-pop ball screen between point guard Gabe Cupps and sixth man Quinn Hafner led to a wide-open three-point shot—a shot Hafner buried, giving us a narrow four-point lead, heading into the final two minutes of our season.

No matter that Centerville High School had never been to a state basketball tournament before. No matter that our team had begun the season unknown and unranked. No matter that the play call with the championship on the line was for a reserve who averaged just over four points per game for the season. Our belief in our process and in each other was unwavering, and now we led by four with only seconds remaining in the state championship game.

But as the final seconds ticked off the clock, our lead and that breathing room melted away point by point. Westerville Central was tough, well coached, and seasoned, with veteran players chasing the same state championship we were. Our initial efforts to hold the ball and run out the clock were ineffective against their pressure defense, leading to a travel and turnover by one of our players. Now in possession of the ball and down by only four points, Central called a timeout to set up a play for a three-point shot. Great execution by them and miscommunication by us led to an open shot by one of their best shooters. He made it, closing the score to a single point, 43–42, with just forty-five seconds remaining. Following a timeout, Central's pressure picked up right where it left off, this time leading to an errant pass, giving the ball back to them and with it a perfect opportunity to win the game. In just over twenty-nine seconds both teams would be judged according to the scoreboard hanging from the ceiling. Right or wrong, that's society's way of gauging success. But it wasn't our way.

People love to keep score. It's everywhere we look. And not just in stadiums, fields, and arenas, but also across every company and industry around the world. In organizations large and small, managers keep score on a whole raft of business metrics: market share, revenue, customer count, growth rate, and profit margin. Even when we aren't at work, our social-media usage has us keeping score by likes, hearts, retweets, followers, and subscriptions.

There is nothing wrong with keeping score. A score is simply a comparison. At best, it offers feedback on our progress and helps us identify our strengths and weaknesses and those of our teams. However, at its worst, keeping score depletes us of our confidence and tempts us to betray our values. At the very moment that trusting our process becomes critical, the scoreboard can inject doubt in even the best-laid plan.

The difference lies in *where the score resides*.

Externally driven scores often leave us feeling like we are never enough. Regardless of how well we perform, we can always find someone doing better, with a bigger house, a superior job, or a more lucrative salary. The continuously moving external scoreboard deems any amount of success insufficient. "What's next?" may seem like a question of aspiration, but it often represents the beginning of the search for the next comparison, one that will leave us with the same feelings of inadequacy.

That said, it would be naive or even ignorant to consider the external scoreboard insignificant. It does matter, but it matters for reasons beyond a futile race for superiority. The feedback we garner from that score is capable of redirecting or reinforcing our actions in the future. It can motivate us to change, or it can encourage us to continue. When emotion is removed and the score is viewed as raw data, the impact of an external scoreboard can be significant. Unfortunately, that's not how we are conditioned to use it.

The outer scoreboard is extrinsic in principle but all too often internal in practice. It serves as proof of our success—money, fame, material possessions, wins—and happiness. Anything that affirms our success and achievement will do. As we succumb to the comparison that an external scoreboard promotes, so do our values and beliefs. Rather than stand out as our own person, we inadvertently become just another member of the status quo, chasing the same illusion society has deemed as success.

But inside, we know something doesn't add up. We know this comparison calls for us to settle for less than we are capable of—less contentment, less fulfillment, less impact. There must be another option. Life must have more to offer than a series of carrots to chase and empty faces to please.

Andrew Carnegie called it "the Judge within." Carnegie, a nineteenth-century steel magnate and philanthropist, was referring to an intrinsic internal scoreboard. He wrote, "The most important judge is yourself. The Judge within sits in the Supreme Court and can never be cheated."[1]

In a speech in 1912, Carnegie explained the importance of living by the rulings of this internal scoreboard. "Having from our own conscience—the Judge within—received a verdict of approval, we have little to fear from any other tribunal."[2] Carnegie attributed this idea for his grand "rule of life" to Scottish poet and national icon Robert Burns, who wrote, "Thine own reproach alone do fear." Carnegie's speech took place at a ceremony unveiling a statue honoring Burns and reflected on the lasting impact these words had on his life: "This motto adopted early in my life has meant more to me than all the sermons I ever heard."[3]

The external scoreboard is outcome driven, while the internal scoreboard is process driven. When we focus on our internal scoreboard, we embrace the reality that we are constantly becoming, never arriving. It's deeply personal and central to who we are as people. Am I living up to my values? Do my behaviors align with what I claim is important to me? Will my habits today provide the impact for my purpose tomorrow? Writer Jack Raines sums it up well in his essay about infinite games. He writes, "The focus on outcome over everything leads to us discounting 99% of our lives for the sake of a few, small, fleeting moments that might provide some sense of satisfaction before the cycle begins anew."[4]

A key question we must ask ourselves in life is: Are we working for an external prize that is beyond our control and often just outside of our grasp, or are we guided by an internal light to become the person we are meant to be? In posing the question, we are merely asking you to consider "the Judge within." It offers freedom and fulfillment that external, outcome-based scoreboards are unable to provide. Coming out on top of our internal scoreboard means we are living in alignment and harmony with our values and purpose. Is that not what life is calling all of us to do?

LIMITATIONS OF THE EXTRINSIC SCOREBOARD

Consider the legacies of Thomas Edison, Abraham Lincoln, Serena Williams, and Warren Buffett. Their inventive work and creative energy changed the world. Had they limited themselves to earning a win as dictated by the external scoreboard, life today would be very different. By focusing on an internal scoreboard, those great innovators were free to dream and create what they envisioned, not simply a better version of someone else's invention.

The same holds true for you.

Living in a world of deficiency is an external-scoreboard obsession. We thrive at identifying what is missing from our lives but present in the lives of others. These thoughts act as brakes working against the drive of our potential. They pull our attention from what *is* here in the present. Under the spell of external scorekeeping, we focus on what we used to have in the past or what we want in the future. We give voice to complaints that diminish the work others have done—"He's so lucky"—or excuse our own failure to do the same—"Sure, you can do that, but it's not so easy for me." In the end, what we have matters less to us than what we don't.

On the other hand, the measuring stick of an internal scoreboard demands that we do the exact opposite. Instead of focusing on what we don't have and can't do, our focus is centered on what we are capable of, what our strengths are, and what our potential can be. Our internal scoreboard eliminates "shoulds" from our lives. It gives us clarity and direction and dramatically impacts the way in which we lead ourselves and others.

KEEPING SCORE FOR TEAMS

All teams are a reflection of their leader, largely influenced by how that leader defines success or the scoreboard they choose to value. It requires intentional coaching and leadership to counterbalance the consistent societal push for comparison. One way to pursue excellence as a team is to be led by a person who pursues excellence first for themselves and then for the team.

This pursuit treats every team as unique. Past teams may provide guidance, especially when the people making up the new team are largely the same. But the past does not set the expectations for the current group. Every single team has its own character, dynamics, and potential. While past teams may be similar, no two are the same. And while past teams may provide guidance, they will never hold the exact same potential as the current one. Each group must be given the space, void of expectation, to become the best team they can be rather than simply another version of a team that came before them.

From this viewpoint, we can see how external goals, like making a certain amount of money, beating a particular rival, or even winning a championship, can end up being as limiting as they are motivating. Preparing to win the conference if the team is capable of winning the national championship seems rather limiting. Preparing to beat a single team on the schedule, regardless of talent level, could easily leave potential untapped. One way to eliminate wasted potential is to remove comparison altogether.

BC: We won the game. Our 2021 State Championship team was a clear example of the power of pursuing excellence, an internal metric, over success, an external one. In our school's history, no basketball team had ever won a regional championship, let alone a state title. Prior to the season, people did not expect us to be the first Centerville boys basketball team to do it. If we had chosen to use an external scoreboard as a goal, we would have aimed short of that. If we had set even an ambitious goal as something just out of our reach, based on historical performance and expectations, that team would never have realized the fullness of its potential. In the process of winning the school's first-ever regional and state championships, we beat the two-time defending state champion and the undefeated, number one–ranked team in the state. Thus began what would end up being a forty-five-game winning streak, one of the longest in the entire country.

I think it's safe to say any external goal we could have set before the season would have been limiting. The internal scoreboard the 2021 team evaluated itself on was a process-oriented goal: "Attack each opportunity with purpose." This was the framework by which we evaluated every workout, every practice, every game, and, ultimately, the entirety of our season. We reflected on it daily and processed the feedback immediately. Critics of intrinsic, process-focused goals like this may say they lead to evaluations that are too subjective, with no empirical evidence to support success or failure. We disagree with the idea that this alone matters. Virtually everything that is truly important in life—happiness, fulfillment, joy, impact, and love—doesn't lend itself to quantification and analysis through numerical data. The 2021 team's commitment to consistently attack opportunities, regardless of how or where they presented themselves, positioned it to keep growing and improving, free from the limits of an external scoreboard that only knows what has been.

Embracing the inner scoreboard is a simple change in how we frame our life and choices. It requires no fancy equipment, technology, or education. It is a simple but very intentional choice to value the score that matters. The payoff is the freedom and fulfillment that external, outcome-based scoreboards fail to provide.

This book is for those looking to become the person they aspire to be rather than the person society repeatedly tells them to be. It's for people ready to approach life differently and choose the path less traveled. It's for those who have tasted the evaporating gratification of success and seek direction toward a more lasting sense of fulfillment and a deeper sense of value in what is truly important. It is for leaders who wish to focus their binoculars on a new perspective and then pass those binoculars to others to share what they're seeing.

The external scoreboard will always exist. Balancing a personal focus on the internal scoreboard with society's prioritization of the external scoreboard is a challenge those striving for excellence must take on. Leadership provides the platform for impact. With our sights clearly focused on what is most important, those we lead will be able to share in the vision. This book is for them, too—not only the leaders who embrace the score that matters but also all the individuals who are impacted by each of those leaders.

HOW THIS BOOK CAME TO BE

This book was born when we began working on projects together and realized the benefits each provides the other. Our ability to merge our experiences and philosophies on leadership has come naturally from the start. Our shared passion for sports and competition is clear, but our congruent view of what excellence looks like is the link that separates ours from other partnerships. We are individuals who share a process-centered approach to leadership that is often dismissed by those focused solely on achievement and results.

BC: I was a quiet fan of Ryan's podcast, *The Learning Leader Show*, and emailed him in hopes that he would speak to our Team Leadership Group (TLG) at Centerville High School, his alma mater. The TLG was composed of leaders from all the school clubs and teams and met once a week. Fellow Centerville basketball coach Eli Leiker and I led the group through various activities and discussions on team leadership. The TLG provided the pathway for me to create the current elective leadership classes Centerville now offers. Ryan was gracious with his time and shared his learnings with the group.

RYAN HAWK (RH): Shortly after I spoke with the TLG, I asked Brook to be one of the guest speakers at my second Learning Leader Growth Summit. The attendees were mostly senior leaders from companies large and small across corporate America. Initially, Brook was hesitant to accept. He said, "What can I possibly teach CEOs and business leaders? They don't want to hear from me." I told him that I thought he could teach them a lot. I was certain that his message would work well off the basketball court. In addition to Brook, I had a handful of other experienced keynote speakers on the agenda. After the workshop was over, I sent a feedback form to all attendees. One of the questions I asked was "Who was your favorite guest speaker?" Brook showed up more than any other name. From that point forward, I asked him to join my Learning Leader Circle, and I've spent many hours working with him to formulate (and live) my core values.

BC: We've become really good friends. Ryan is one of my foxhole guys that I trust and talk to about questions and ways to think about life in general. Since that original talk years ago, we've conducted a lot of leadership workshops together. Ryan's genuine curiosity stretches me. Every time I'm with him, he makes me better. His pursuit of growth and excellence encourages me to fight complacency and continue down a path of improvement. As we've worked more together, we've learned that we're very aligned when it comes to leadership and living a life of excellence.

RH: When I interviewed economics professor and best-selling author Tyler Cowen, he told me, "If you have an opportunity to work with someone who is awesome and brilliant who will cooperate with you, you should always do that. Drop everything and do that." After publishing two books by myself, I was asked if I would ever write with someone else. I always said, "No, it's too personal." I have since changed my mind.

Brook is a world-class leader. I admire what he's accomplished and, more importantly, how he's done it. Brook has led his teams to many wins, but his impact goes far beyond what happens on the court. The mark of an excellent leader is that they build more leaders. That's what Brook has done in spades. I believe he's only scratched the surface on the number of people he will impact in his life.

Most books are the result of the wisdom of one author and one set of experiences. This one is the result of two people who have been on a rigorous decades-long mission to deconstruct excellence wherever it is found. We'll lay it all on the table in both a descriptive and prescriptive manner. We'll zoom out to the 30,000-foot view of why developing yourself as a leader is essential, and we'll zoom in to share the tactics, behaviors, and actions you can deploy to do the inner work to become transformational leaders. This book is a distillation of actions, behaviors, and practical applications for our daily lives. While it presents philosophical ideas that will propel you to question yourself and your beliefs, it is packed with specific actions to take, exercises to use, and tools to analyze what works best. What should you continue to do and what should you stop? Transformational leaders live lives full of experiments, and we want to inspire you to do just that.

We share this material in our Learning Leader Circles (paid mastermind groups). We teach it to corporate clients. We use it to win championships. We have given hundreds of keynote speeches all over the world and regularly work with professional coaches and front-office executives from the National College Athletic Association, the National Football League, the National Basketball Association, and Major League Baseball. We advise CEOs and senior executives from billion-dollar companies and small businesses alike. The ideas in this book have been stress-tested. We have carefully documented what resonates and is effective in living a life aimed at pursuing excellence. This is the best of the best. The information in this book is what we share with our clients. Now we are sharing it with you. Let's get started.

CHAPTER 1
You Lie Too Much

*The world has always been full of sheep. You want to be
a sheep, okay, this is a democracy.*

*But if you want to find your own way, this is the time
to do it. It's not harder to be yourself, it's just more obvious that it's hard. Really hard. It's always been hard.*

—Jane Campion

In Lewis Carroll's classic tale of the girl who fell down the rabbit
hole, Alice finds herself shrunken after swallowing some pebble-
turned-cake. Looking for something to counteract its effect and return
to her normal size, Alice searches among the tall grass and towering
flowers of a garden until she comes to a large mushroom. Standing on
her tiptoes, Alice is barely able to peer over the side of it but sees a big
caterpillar seated atop. After a period of awkward silence, the caterpillar takes a long drag on a hookah pipe and asks, "Who are *you*?"

"I—I hardly know, Sir," says Alice, "just at present—at least I know who I *was* when I got up this morning, but I think I must have been changed several times since then."[1]

Such is the path of self-awareness. It begins with the knowledge that you hardly know yourself, given the fleeting glances in the proverbial mirror we take as we move through the hustle and bustle of our modern lives. In our experience, self-awareness is a foundational piece that leaders often overlook. We have to know ourselves prior to leading others. In developing as a leader, it's easy to assume that we already possess the kind of self-awareness that's necessary, but let's be honest: we don't have it, and we never really will have it completely. Real self-awareness is something we will always be working on. Building it is a never-ending process.

Without a finish line, people tend to want to skip the work of developing self-awareness. It's hard. But to be secure in what we're doing, we have to first figure out who we are. Taking a cold, hard look at ourselves in the mirror and reflecting on what we've screwed up or what we need to change is not easy. It is a difficult process—but it's worth it.

Self-awareness is the only trailhead for the path to excellence. Sure, people may be successful and gain fame, glory, and riches without it, but they won't experience excellence. Excellence requires authenticity, and authenticity requires self-awareness. The question isn't "Do you want to do the work to be self-aware?" It's "Do you want to pursue excellence?" If the answer is yes, then self-awareness is the first step.

The challenge with self-awareness, of course, is that we aren't good at it. Organizational psychologist and author Tasha Eurich reports[2] that while 95 percent of people think they are self-aware, only 10–15 percent of them actually are. Therefore, while becoming self-aware is challenging, realizing we are *not* self-aware seems to be the root issue. After all, why would we seek something we think we already have? We don't look for the keys to the car when we think we have them in our pocket. No, that panic is reserved for the moment we realize we don't have them. The same is true for our self-awareness. Unfortunately, the realization of the need for self-awareness typically requires the pain of desperation that comes from a specific form of failure: when the destined-for-success vision of who we think we are collides with a harsh reality that fails to align. Hitting that proverbial rock bottom (sometimes more than once) is what compels us to take a deep look into ourselves. With curiosity and humility, we are forced to be honest about what we see. To forget who everyone wants us to be; to forget who society tells us we should be. At rock bottom, we see who we truly are.

GUEST EVALUATORS

BC: Because of the disparity between how many of us think we are self-aware and how many actually are, getting insight from outside our own heads is critical. When you are deeply entrenched in something, it can be hard to see it clearly. In those cases, I believe it's important to create a system that can provide the awareness and clarity that we need to continue improving.

For this reason, I invite people to observe our basketball practices throughout the year. I'm very selective about who I invite. I don't care what anyone in general thinks, but I do care about what a certain kind of person thinks: the kind who understands high standards, knows what it takes to live by them, and is willing to tell me the truth about what they see. These people touch excellence in some way. I invite them, even if they don't know anything about basketball. They don't need to. The feedback they are invited to provide is about our *how*, not our *what*. Each guest receives an evaluation form that I ask them to fill out throughout the practice with the following questions:

- What are the first words that come to mind when you watch these individual players practice? (I provide a roster of our players.)
- Based on what you observed, what are two things we are focused on being great at?
- What two things did you like best about our culture? What two things would you change?
- What is the first word or phrase that comes to mind when you watch our whole team practice?

I believe if we are properly emphasizing and living our values, they should be apparent to anyone watching our practice, whether or not that person knows the difference between a man-to-man defense and a 1-3-1 defense. Their outsider observations help me and the other coaches assess whether our rhetorical focus on values is materializing in our daily actions in practice. These guests are invaluable for providing us with a better picture of who we really are and where we need to go.

USE FEAR AS FUEL

Every student who passes through Centerville's leadership class is asked to answer a deceptively simple question: "What's holding you back?" Year in and year out, fear of failure is the most common answer.

One way to deal with the fear of failure is to reframe how you think about the situation by choosing to focus on the things you can control. You may not be able to change much about an external situation, but you have full control over your attitude, mentality, and response. By doing this, you unlock the ability to transform your fear from an obstacle into fuel.

RH: I have been afraid of failing my whole life. When my high-school football coaches told me I was going to play quarterback on the varsity team as a freshman, my overriding emotion wasn't excitement or pride. It was fear. I was afraid to let my coaches and teammates down.

That fear was as much a part of my uniform as my helmet and shoulder pads when I ran onto the field for the first game of the season against Cincinnati Oak Hills. I was fourteen years old and had yet to step foot inside Centerville High School as a student—that first game was on the Friday night before the school year started.

With about five minutes left in the game, we got the ball. We were behind by four points and needed a touchdown to win—and we did it. My first-ever high-school touchdown pass was a twenty-yard throw to Neal Laabs, a junior running back, that secured a 38–36 win for us. Though I earned a temporary high, I continued to be scared to fail and let people down each time I stepped on the field, whether in high school, in college, or as a professional player.

When I graduated from college, the uncertainty of what I was going to do with my life left me fearful. When I got my first office job, I had a deep fear that I would let down the family friend who had hired me. When I launched my podcast, I did so in the face of fears that I would sound like an idiot and embarrass myself. When I signed up to do a triathlon, I was scared I would drown in the open water of Ohio's Delaware Lake. After signing my first book deal, I feared that, after reading my first draft, my editor at McGraw Hill would realize she had made a big mistake.

I've been fearful hundreds of times before going onstage to deliver a big keynote speech. Right before you go onstage—just as they're introducing you to the audience—you have a moment to yourself for a little self-talk. It can set the tone for how the speech goes—for you as the speaker, but especially for the audience.

I can go on and on. Fear has been an ever-present feature of my life. I feel it all the time, and I think that's a good thing. It's a signal that I care. And I use it. I use the fear of failure as fuel. I use that fear to push myself to be overprepared. I use that fear as fuel to perform well when it matters most.

I know I'm not the only one. Cody Keenan first began working for President Barack Obama before Obama was president. Keenan started out as an intern in the Chicago headquarters of Obama's first presidential campaign. Once the campaign was over, Keenan followed the newly elected president to the White House, eventually serving as the director of speechwriting. It was in that capacity where Keenan earned the nickname "Hemingway" from President Obama. With a BA from Northwestern University and a master's degree from Harvard University's John F. Kennedy School of Government, Keenan's professional exploits shouldn't come as a surprise. Given his credentials, it was surprising to hear from him the role fear has played in his success.

Of that time serving as President Obama's chief speechwriter, Keenan told me, "I was afraid a lot . . . I was always afraid of letting him down [or] writing something that was subpar." Despite being handpicked by President Obama to serve in that role, Keenan wrestled with the self-doubts of imposter syndrome. "I never felt like I deserved to be there, so there was also this fear of being found out as a fraud."[3]

We often think of the fears of self-doubt and of not measuring up as bad vibes that can be debilitating in the pursuit of excellence. But they need not be. "Fear can actually be a powerful motivator," Keenan told me. "I was always so afraid to fail [Obama], and the American people, and the people whose stories we were telling, that I would pull all-nighters to make sure the speech sang . . . I would work weekends to make sure a draft sang."

What does Keenan say to those who preach that people shouldn't be afraid to fail? He doesn't mince words. "I disagree with that," he told me. It echoed the message he delivered to the graduates of New York University's Wagner Graduate School of Public Service at their 2015 commencement: "You should ignore that advice. You should be so afraid of failure that you're willing to do anything to succeed . . . Fear of failure keeps you sharp, even if it keeps you sleepless. It's why, for weeks before something like the State of the Union Address, my car is the last one in the parking lot at night. I'm afraid all the time. I'm afraid to let my colleagues see that I'm not as smart as they are. I'm afraid to let the President down."[4]

In his book *Think Like a Monk*, author Jay Shetty argues for seeing fear in a new light: as a beacon pointing the way toward opportunity. He writes, "What we should really fear is that we will miss the opportunities that fear offers . . . Our fear of fear is what holds us back."[5]

According to Shetty, fear is just one of four primary motivators at work in the human psyche. Fear has its place alongside desire (the pursuit of personal gratification through success, wealth, and pleasure), duty (the urge to do the right thing out of a sense of responsibility or appreciation), and love (an appetite for helping others arising from a sense of caring for them). Rarely are our actions motivated purely from just one of these things. We are typically moved to action by multiple motivators, either simultaneously or in rapid-fire succession. Fear can be used as a great ignition source in almost all situations. But like the kindling you use to start a campfire, fear can't keep burning at its brightest for a long period of time. A longer-burning, more sustaining fuel is required for the long haul.

RH: Take something as simple as my fear heading into a big keynote speech. The motivation I have to deliver an excellent experience draws from each of the four motivators. Because I am constantly exercising my willingness to embrace challenges, fear of failing is the one I feel first. This fear ignites in me the drive not just to prepare to do well but also to overprepare. I feel the same productive paranoia when preparing for a keynote speech as I do when preparing for each new podcast episode. I've learned over time that if I don't embrace that fear, harness it, and direct it toward productive preparation, it will drag me into shutting down, procrastinating, and ultimately experiencing the very failure I am afraid of.

As I start moving along the path of preparation and become more familiar with the audience that I will be serving, a new motivation takes shape. The desire to be seen in a positive light by those who hired me emerges. The human ego is never void of being motivated by desire, and I'm no exception. Whether it ends up coming in the form of verbal compliments, social-media likes, or the monetary value of higher speaking rates, being liked by members of the community is a powerfully motivating desire.

Duty and love are the longest burning of the motivational fuels, and for me, they kick into gear as I gain a full understanding of what I am being asked to deliver, to whom, and why. With a clear picture of the purpose of the keynote address and the impact it could have on the attendees in the room (not to mention the potential ripple effect on those who will end up hearing about my talk secondhand), a deep sense of responsibility to do the job for which I was hired to the best of my ability arises. Love for the people in the audience who are giving me their time and attention kicks in, driving me to serve them with the most impactful message I can possibly deliver. That I am willing to take risks to deliver an A+ performance rather than just playing it safe and giving a perfectly acceptable B+/A- experience is a function of that motivation. It is an act of generosity to do more work than necessary to deliver a better outcome than required. Whenever you see someone doing that for someone else, that is the motivation of love at work.

By this point in my process, fear as a motivator will simply be passing thoughts of inferiority that provide occasional jolts of focus. Useful as bursts of corrective energy, for sure, but it will ultimately be overshadowed by the sustainability of motivation through duty and love.

A desire to better understand ourselves coupled with a willingness to confront fear head-on are vital to moving toward a focus on the score that matters. Here are a few valuable exercises.

────────────────── TAKE ACTION ──────────────────

Exercise: Letter to Your Younger Self

Why: To increase self-awareness

How: Write a letter to your ten-year-old self. What's important? What risks would you encourage your younger self to take? What should they not worry about?

Exercise: Fear of Failure

Why: To confront fear

How: Make a table with three columns. Label column one "Fear," column two "Solution," and column three "Bet."

1. List your fears in column one.
2. Describe the outcome you would bet on in column three.
3. Write down the basic solution for the fear you are experiencing in column two. (It's important to do this last.)

Example:

Fears	Simple Solution	Outcome Bet
Letting down coach	He wants my best, not perfection	He will still trust me
Public speaking	Overprepare; three breaths; go for it	I'll do well, like usual

CHAPTER 2

Life ~~or~~ and Death

I wish everyone could get rich and famous and get every-thing they ever dreamed of so they can see that's not the answer.

—Jim Carrey

Where are you going?" It's a fairly elementary question. We tend to think of it in terms of known destinations: either to work or returning home; to an appointment at a particular time and place; to an address entered into the GPS app on our phone. Have you ever been in a car with someone who had directions to their destination but could not tell you which *direction* they were facing at any given moment? Everything is fine so long as nothing unexpected happens and the next turn listed in the directions arrives as promised and is clearly recognizable. Of course, when a wrinkle shows up in the plan—an error in the directions, a missing landmark, or a forced detour—then something remarkable happens. A huge gap opens up between what is supposed to happen and what *is* happening—where you are supposed to be going versus where you are.

When it comes to how we live our lives, navigating by a destination address is a recipe for frustration and failure. The uncertainty of what lies beyond the fleeting moment of the present can make a mess out of even the most detailed of future plans. In life, what is needed is not a set destination. We need a north star, rather than an address, to guide us. Maps aren't that helpful for navigating the future. But a compass might be.

There is a beautiful elegance to the simplicity of how a compass works. All one needs is a lightweight magnet set to move on a frictionless swivel. From there, the laws of magnetic attraction take over. The needle is free to spin in any direction, allowing the opposing pole of the magnet to point in the direction of the north pole of Earth's magnetic field.

Author Steven Pressfield encourages anyone pursuing a noble goal worth doing to use the resistance they feel as their compass. He writes, "Like a magnetized needle floating on a surface of oil, Resistance will unfailingly point to true North—meaning that call or action it most wants to stop us from doing. We can use this. We can use it as a compass. We can navigate by Resistance, letting it guide us to that calling or action that we must follow before all others."[1]

While there is no denying the value of Pressfield's perspective, the true North that *our* compass points to is different. The direction we are forever aiming at is not defined by what opposes us but by what fuels us. For us, that is our passion. And we don't mean the standard "follow your passion and you'll never work a day in your life" advice that is spewed so often. In fact, passion is all about work.

The word *passion* comes from the Latin word *passio,* the literal definition of which is "suffering" or "enduring." It is the struggle that makes something your passion—your willingness to endure, to keep going, to suffer. All of that makes up a passion. The hard is what makes it good.

It's hard to consistently publish an excellent podcast episode every week for nine years, especially if your bar for quality increases all the time. It is hard to send an email newsletter 350 weeks in a row without fail. We all have the same hard stuff (family, work stresses, etc.). We must be willing to endure and even embrace the suffering because it's worth it. It's worth it to talk with and learn from amazing leaders. It's worth it to see the impact our work has on others. Passion is about the hard stuff. If you're not willing to suffer and endure, then you will do what most people do: quit. The right questions are "What will I endure? What is worth the pain? What am I willing to make sacrifices for?"

Writing this book is a prime example. It was a grind. There were many days when we didn't feel like doing it, but we knew the result would be worth it. The chance to impact people's lives made that struggle worth it. As best-selling author and renowned speaker Donald Miller told us when we visited with him in Nashville, "Writing a book is like climbing a mountain in the fog. You don't know where the top is, but if you walk uphill every morning for two hours, you're going to get there."

To find the motivation to push through the adversity that a true passion requires, you must have a rock-solid answer to the question your inner voice will scream at you: *Why are you doing this?* Or, put another way: *What is your purpose?* We have all had to face that question. It is almost impossible to keep pushing forward and endure the suffering of a passion if you don't have a handle on your purpose for doing so.

Ask Jack Wiemar. Prior to the start of a game in the Oxford Regional of the 2018 NCAA college baseball championship tournament, Ole Miss head coach Mike Bianco gathered his players around him and told them Wiemar's story. Wiemar suffered from chronic obesity, having tried and failed to lose weight several times. Doctors began warning him that, at over three hundred pounds, he was putting himself at great risk of an early death from a heart attack or stroke. Despite this powerful motivator, Wiemar continued to be unsuccessful at following through on his commitment to a healthier diet and fit lifestyle.

"And then one day he got some bad news," Coach Bianco told his team. Wiemar's daughter, Megan, was diagnosed with a rare kidney disease and would need a transplant to survive. Of all the family members tested for compatibility, only Wiemar's results came back positive. This, of course, was exciting news for Wiemar, who was more than eager to give his kidney to save the life of his daughter. But Wiemar's obesity stood in the way. Megan's doctors would not approve her father as a donor because of the risk to his life that the surgery would entail. Additionally, they would not put the kidney of an unhealthy person into someone of such fragile health as Megan.

Faced with this bittersweet news, Wiemar asked the doctors how much time Megan could wait for the transplant if he were to work on getting himself healthy enough to be her donor. They estimated maybe six months. With this new sense of purpose, Wiemar found the commitment to doing the hard work of getting healthy that had eluded him for all those years. In just six months, he succeeded in losing one hundred pounds and was able to successfully donate his kidney to his daughter.[2] That's how much difference a firm grasp of purpose can make.

Why does someone teach and coach? Why does someone give keynote speeches or record a podcast? Why do we parent? Here's what answering those questions sounds like for us.

BC: My purpose is to inspire others to strive for excellence over success. I define success as a comparison to others, while excellence is the best possible version of yourself. Unfortunately, much of society is

deeply invested in the comparison of success. As a high-school teacher
and coach, I see the dangers of this comparison firsthand: from the
frustration of chasing the highest GPA to the devastation of feeling like
a failure for not earning a Division I scholarship. It's never-ending and
fleetingly fulfilling. Anyone who's ever accomplished what seems to be
a major achievement will quickly acknowledge the transient nature of
the satisfaction of being on top. We almost immediately begin thinking, *That's it?* And then, *What's next?* We think we want the top of the
podium when what we really want is the feeling we think the top of the
podium will provide.

The pursuit of success ultimately leaves us feeling empty. Sure, we
may have won some trophies and earned some awards, but who have
we become in that process? Who we become as a result of the striving is
what excellence is all about. Comparison leads to judgment. Excellence
doesn't judge. Excellence works. It struggles. It fails. And it tries again.
Excellence is marked by scars on the outside but filled with hope, confidence, and belief on the inside. True fulfillment will always be just out
of grasp to those longing for success, while those pursuing excellence
can enjoy it daily.

RH: I am motivated to inspire others to *value* and pursue excellence.
To me, excellence is about going to bed a little bit wiser than when
you woke up. It's about pushing yourself beyond your current limits to
broaden your current capabilities. It's expanding your zone of comfort
and competency. I try to do this through how I approach my work. I
value consistency, curiosity, thoughtfulness, and being thankful for the
gifts that I've been given. I'm also motivated by the privilege that I was
born into. I have two amazing parents. I have two brothers who are as
supportive as brothers get. I am so fortunate to partner with a wife who
is always there for me. My parents worked hard and provided a great
life for our family; they continue to do that to this day. I am motivated

to make the absolute most out of what I've been given. I don't want to waste that gift. As I get older and talk with more people, I realize that many didn't have the upbringing that was just normal for me. I believe that when you're given a lot, you should give a lot. I think about that every day. I hope that by the end of my time, people who know me will say I gave more than I got. And I've received a lot. It's an ambitious goal—one that is hard to measure but on my mind all the time.

To articulate our purpose, we must first clarify what we aspire to. Striving for championships and promotions is a fire that burns hot but burns quick. As a fuel, it doesn't last. Destination-based goals just don't provide the sense of fulfillment we long for in a life well lived.

In this light, we quickly realize that a purpose requires others. It's less about us and more about the people we communicate with, interact with, and serve. What do we desire our impact on others to be? How are they better for having known us? People rarely consider these questions, but they may be the most important questions of our lives.

Once we navigate through this labyrinth and uncover our desired impact, we must consider our part in making it a reality. Clearly, our desired impact isn't achieved simply by other people knowing us. It requires us to take specific measures and actions to ensure others are moved to the feelings and behaviors we are hoping for. What are those behaviors? What will you do to create the greatest likelihood that your desired impact will occur? When our words match our actions, we are aligned with our purpose. Our critical behaviors allow us to fulfill our values. By fulfilling our values, we fulfill our purpose. Your purpose touches everything in your life. It's not compartmentalized into work-you and home-you or parent-you and friend-you. Alignment and authenticity are the ultimate goals.

WHY WE SHOULD THINK ABOUT DEATH

Author Michael Easter is on a mission to convince people that discomfort is the key to living a happier, better life. Easter's research took him to the tiny Asian country of Bhutan. Nestled in the Himalayas, between China to its north and India to its south, Bhutan has a population roughly equal to that of North Dakota in a quarter of the land area. Technologically, as Easter said on *The Learning Leader Show*, "Bhutan is one of the least developed countries on earth. The entire country does not have a stoplight."[3] Life in that environment is hard by definition. Despite this, Bhutan consistently ranks in the top twenty countries of the happiest people, according to researchers in Japan who study happiness. Easter traveled to Bhutan to find out why.

Surprisingly, a huge part of the answer lies in Bhutan's cultural focus on death. That culture is heavily influenced by Buddhism, which is the country's official religion and the religious identification of roughly 85 percent of Bhutan's population. For practitioners of Buddhism, death is one of the most important aspects of life, and an intentional focus on its inevitability is key to enlightenment and the happiness that comes from it. Bhutanese culture stresses the importance of intentionally thinking about death at least once a day.

"Death is sort of baked into the culture in a lot of ways," Easter noted. It seemed to him that everywhere he looked there were visual reminders of death in the form of tiny little bell-shaped cones about three inches tall. These clay creations, known as *tsa tsa*, can be seen along the sides of roads, in windowsills, or stacked on rocks all across the country. The clay used to make them comes from combining mud with the ashes of the dead collected from funeral pyres. "There's this constant reminder that this ride is going to end," Easter said.

The point of all of this focus on death for the people of Bhutan isn't to be morbid, sad, or uncomfortable. That is a creation of Western culture, particularly in America. "Think about our funeral system," Easter said. "People are immediately put into the ground. We're told, 'Take your mind off it. Keep yourself busy. You don't want to think about it.'" In forcing oneself to think about the inevitability and universality of death—you can't avoid it, and nobody is immune to it—the result is alignment. "You start to think about *What really matters to me?*" said Easter. "Because if I know this ride is going to end, I'm not going to spend it worked up about this random email I got from someone I work with that tends to piss me off. I'm going to spend more time with my wife and kids." The end result of this focus on death is that people tend to change their behavior, and an increase in happiness follows.

One of our favorite self-awareness exercises to help you discover where you want to go is memorializing yourself. In other words, sit down and write your own eulogy. It makes you think about why you work to build a sturdy foundation, how you want to impact others, and where you want to go with a more important perspective in mind. Imagine what people might say about you after you're gone. Are people going to talk about you being the CEO, or the amount of money you made, or how many social-media followers you had? Probably not. Like it or not, considering how you will be remembered is powerful. It's especially powerful if there is a gap between how you would currently be remembered and how you want to be remembered. The aspirational script is the guide for your true self.

The world encourages us to base everything on our résumé. That's how we're rewarded. That's how society is structured. If we aren't intentional about breaking that mold, we will inevitably be shaped by it. If we never adopt a different mindset, we will wander through life without thinking. That becomes our identity by default. If we never go through this process of self-reflection, we will never acquire the tools necessary to be able to articulate our beliefs and values to ourselves. We will fall into patterns that other people create for us rather than patterns we create for ourselves.

———————————— TAKE ACTION ————————————

Exercise: Write Your Eulogy

Why: To allow the reality of death to provide conviction for your purpose

How: Write your eulogy in twenty-four words or less for simplicity and clarity.

Exercise: Your Purpose

Why: To become clear and intentional

How: Write a single sentence with two parts in answer to these questions:

1.   What will you do to impact those around you? (Inspire, model, create, etc.)
2.   What do you hope others will do as a result of your actions?

Example:

BC: *Inspire others to pursue excellence over success.*
RH: *Inspire others to value and pursue excellence.*

CHAPTER 3

Fate Is a Terrible Writer

Authentic happiness derives from raising the bar for yourself, not rating yourself against others.

—Martin Seligman

Growing up in rural Ohio, learning to drive meant more than understanding the difference between the brake and the gas pedal or between a stop sign and a yield sign. When directions are more likely to reference landmarks than street names, paying attention to the scenery can be critically important. "Turn left at the big red barn, and it'll be down there by the oak tree on the right."

It's important to understand the difference between being a passenger and a driver. The passenger is free to pay no attention to anything while the driver must observe everything. Sitting in the back seat means you can sleep through several hundred miles of road without any issue. You will get to your destination regardless of your level of

situational awareness and participation. You share none of the responsibility for getting there, let alone for getting there safely.

Things are very different for the person behind the wheel. The
driver must be present and focused at all times. Responsibility for the
safety of everyone in their car rests upon the driver's shoulders. In fact,
that responsibility extends beyond the vehicle itself, as the driver owes a
moral and legal duty to the other drivers and pedestrians in the immediate area. The driver must take ownership of and be accountable for all
of that. Why? The driver has power. Passengers do not.

This distinction explains the differences between how the Soviet
Union and NASA designed space capsules at the dawn of the space age
in the 1960s. When Soviet cosmonaut Yuri Gagarin became the first
human to orbit the earth on April 12, 1961, he did so in a spherical
capsule called Vostok 1. This flying ball had no control inputs for the
human inside. All of its flight systems—for orienting the capsule for
reentry and for firing its retro-rockets for the braking thrust needed
to reenter the Earth's atmosphere—were controlled by automated programs. The only aspect of the flight Gagarin could influence at all was
pushing a single button that would trigger the reentry program to run
early in case of an emergency. Gagarin was a pilot in name only; in
reality, he was merely a passenger on his 106-minute flight into history.

The Soviet mindset was reflected in the design: the prominence of
the system over the individual meant that the role of a human pilot
was minimized. In contrast, the Americans intentionally designed
their spacecraft to "make the astronaut a central figure in the operation
of the spacecraft, especially in his ability to veto automatic systems."[1]
Like the Vostok 1, the blunt cone-shaped Mercury capsule flew and
fell ballistically (like a bullet, with no ability to generate lift or change
direction in flight), and its systems also executed automated programs
to manage its performance through the flight plan. But unlike Gagarin,
the Mercury astronauts had the ability to override the program and

veto the computer's intended action. In this design scheme, the human being in the spacecraft was "an invaluable part of the space flight systems as pilot, engineer and experimenter."[2]

This distinction came into sharp focus on America's first orbital flight. On February 20, 1962, NASA launched the third manned mission of Project Mercury with Ohioan John Glenn aboard the spacecraft designated *Friendship 7*. After the first of Glenn's three planned orbits, controllers on the ground noticed the altitude positioning of the spacecraft was off. As designed, the automated systems kicked in, using a burst of propellant from a control thruster to correct it. But the drift persisted, and each automated correction used up more of the ship's limited supply of propellant. At that point, Glenn intervened: he took hold of the control stick and manually kept the spacecraft pointed in the right direction, reducing the use of precious propellant in the process. "He was a pilot, by training and temperament, and pilots take control."[3]

Passengers do not.

It is hard to overstate how dramatic this shift in mindset is. Brook saw it up close when teaching his son, Gabe, to drive. Suddenly, his son's favorite car activity—sleeping—was no longer an option. The same applies to the journey of life. There are times when we need to trust someone else to drive and our job is to be the best passenger we can be: supportive, helpful, and there for the driver. But ultimately, the people who are making a dent in the world and trying to make a difference over the long haul are the ones who love the responsibility of being in the driver's seat.

What that distinction between driver and passenger really gets at is the difference between having an internal locus of control and having an external one. Donald Miller is a best-selling author and the CEO of StoryBrand. At our leadership retreat in Nashville, Tennessee, he defined having an internal locus of control as believing that "for the most part, I am in charge of my own well-being." This driver mentality plays a key role in achieving better life outcomes. According to Miller, psychological studies have shown that "people who have adopted an internal locus of control are happier; they make more money; they have better marriages; they have better relationships; they experience less anxiety, less clinical depression."[4]

In contrast, an external locus of control is a mindset that sees all of the causes of one's success and well-being as being beyond one's reach and control: "I have no bearing on my well-being. The bearing that affects my well-being or that plays upon it would be the government, or God, or fate." Miller continued, "I am somebody who believes in God, but I believe that God gives us more of a locus of control than we think. A lot of the crap that happens in our life is because of ourselves. When you accept that, you also get to accept control and direction in your life."

An external locus of control is at the heart of a victim mindset. In this way of thinking, things continually happen *to* you, whether good or bad, and you are powerless to influence those outcomes one way or the other. It is a posture of helplessness and hopelessness. Those who live in this space too long begin finding ways of making it work to their benefit. Seeking sympathy and gaining favor with others through pity may feel good in the short term, but it leads straight to a narcissistic personality that is poisonous to leadership and excellence of any kind.

To say we should adopt a posture of an internal locus of control is not to say that external circumstances and environmental realities don't have a role to play in our life's outcomes. Of course they do. Still, it is important to recognize how internal factors within us interact with external forces.

Performance coach Tim Kight describes this relationship in the form of a simple equation that drew national attention during the 2015 national championship run of the Ohio State Buckeyes football team.

After a chance meeting with then–head coach Urban Meyer, Kight spent two years drilling his leadership principle of "E + R = O" into players and coaches alike. When the team won the College Football Playoff championship, the third-string quarterback who led it to its playoff victories wore an "E + R = O" wristband while doing so.[5]

When Kight appeared on *The Learning Leader Show*, he explained the variables at work: "E" are the events that occur in your life. "R" is your response to those events. And "O" is the outcome produced when the event is combined with your response. The focus of the R factor is to spend our time and energy on the one thing we actually have control over: our response to the events in our lives.[6]

Poor drivers are notorious for becoming consumed with events that happen to them, like being cut off in traffic, and for allowing their emotions to determine their response. These events push them out of the driver's seat of their life. Their locus of control shifts from internal to external. While still physically driving their car, they are emotionally just along for the ride. When this happens, they end up headed for an outcome they do not want. As Miller puts it, "I don't think any of us should trust fate to write the story of our lives. Fate is a terrible writer."

"WE'RE ON TO CINCINNATI"

Heading into the 2014 NFL season, the New England Patriots were struggling through a ten-year string of frustration. During that span of time, they'd made it back to the Super Bowl twice only to lose both times to the New York Giants. Three other seasons had ended with losses in the AFC Championship Game. After winning three Super Bowls in four years between 2001 and 2004, the Patriots looked like a team that had reached the summit of pro football enough times that they no longer had what it took to do it again.

Four weeks into the new season, on a Monday night in Kansas City at the end of September, it looked that way to all of America. The 41–14 loss to the Kansas City Chiefs was an organizational humiliation. For the first time in his career, Tom Brady was benched late in the game not for rest but due to poor play. "Embarrassing MNF Blowout Loss to Chiefs Sounds Death Knell for Patriots Dynasty," proclaimed sports news site Bleacher Report.[7] "We have no idea about the character of this group, but if it's anything close to what we've watched over the first four games," wrote Eric Wilbur of Boston.com, "it has one characteristic never before attached to a Bill Belichick-coached Patriots team. Hopelessness."[8]

Two days later, Belichick began his weekly press conference with an opening statement. Each of its 214 words focused on one thing: the Patriots' next opponent, the undefeated Cincinnati Bengals.[9] The first two media questions yielded another Bengal-focused 258 words from Belichick. Then one of the reporters tried to ask him about what the past—the loss to the Chiefs—meant for the Patriots' future. The question gave birth to one of the more iconic moments in coaching press-conference history.

> **Q:** Your team has been successful for so long. How difficult is it to adjust to the adversity of Monday night's game and get back on track? This team and organization hasn't had these sort of issues in the past.
>
> **BB:** We're on to Cincinnati.
>
> **Q:** You mentioned Tom Brady's age at the draft—
>
> **BB:** We're on to Cincinnati.
>
> **Q:** Do you think having a thirty-seven-year-old—
>
> **BB:** We're on to Cincinnati. It's nothing about the past, nothing about the future. Right now we're preparing for Cincinnati.
>
> **Q:** Do you think the talent you have here is good?

BB: We're getting ready for Cincinnati.

Q: Do you think you've done enough to help Tom Brady?

BB: We're getting ready for Cincinnati. That's what we're doing.

Belichick's mantra of ignoring both the past and the future and focusing only on the present paid dividends. By the end of the 2014 season, the Patriots had won their fourth Super Bowl title. Two years later, they won their fifth. During a press conference at an off-season minicamp in 2017, the coach was asked what goals he had left on his personal checklist as he prepared to enter his eighteenth season leading the Patriots.

"I'd like to go out and have a good practice today. That would be at the top of the list right now," the coach responded. "Okay, but what about after that?" followed up the reporter. "We'll correct it and get ready for tomorrow," said Belichick.[10]

Belichick's focus on the daily process—on the act of practicing with excellence—is what has led to his extraordinary results. His teams haven't won because he set ambitious goals; they have won because they set a standard of excellence for how to behave each day. Their focus is on doing the next repetition as well as they possibly can—and when they have done that, they do the next one. Those reps stack up day after day. Eventually, we all see the results on Super Bowl Sunday at the end of the year. The Patriots made it back to the Super Bowl again in 2017, losing to the Eagles in a dramatic game. That next spring, they got back to work focusing only on the present. By the time February rolled around, there were the Patriots and Bill Belichick, hoisting their sixth Vince Lombardi Trophy.

The importance of living in the present moment is quite simple: it's the only one we can control. We can reflect on and discuss how the game went last night, but it's over. We can't do anything about it now. We can project and imagine the games to come, but they're not here yet. The future is, however, contingent on one thing: the present. Each choice we make in the present leads us to a specific point in the future. The simplicity of it is both empowering and debilitating: empowering because excellence is always at our fingertips, and debilitating because mediocrity is, too.

In the present moment, there is no sadness or depression from regret, and there is no nervousness or anxiety for the future. The present moment just is. Excellence lives in this judgment-free zone of the present. This mindset is reflected in the wisdom of Marcus Aurelius, emperor of ancient Rome and among the most well-known Stoic philosophers. Author Ryan Holiday explained on *The Learning Leader Show* how his outlook frees you from the stresses of emotion that arise out of focusing on either the past or the future:[11]

> Don't let your reflection on the whole sweep of life crush you. Don't fill your mind with all the bad things that might still happen. Stay focused on the present situation. Seize the present moment. Don't get distracted. Don't dwell on regret, don't give in to anxiety. Look at what is in front of you with everything you have. The present moment is the same for everyone, regardless of their job, no matter how well or bad things have been going. The present is all anyone possesses. To waste it, to let it escape you, to let fear or frustration take over is not only how to set yourself up for failure but also a rejection of a beautiful gift.

IT'S ALL QUALITY TIME

Being focused on the present isn't just a strategy for winning football games. How we view the time we have in our hands *right now* dictates how we succeed at and enjoy life itself. Legendary comedian Jerry Seinfeld has a great take on the value of the present:[12]

I'm a believer in the ordinary and the mundane. These guys that talk about "quality time"—I always find that a little sad when they say, "We have quality time." I don't want quality time. I want the garbage time. That's what I like. You just see [your kids] in their room reading a comic book and you get to kind of watch that for a minute, or [having] a bowl of Cheerios at eleven o'clock at night when they're not even supposed to be up. The garbage, that's what I love.

RH: Last December, I was walking around next to a parking lot, listening to a podcast as I waited for my daughter Ella to finish practice for her high-school dance team. Another dad who was waiting for his daughter approached me. He's a nice guy: quiet, smart, has a good job, and supports his family.

I took my AirPods out as we struck up a conversation, doing the usual awkward dad thing of talking with someone you only know from seeing them at school events, which inevitably involves small talk about our kids. I shared how Miranda, my wife, and I were so busy with our kids' sports: taking them to tournaments, staying in hotels, serving as Uber drivers for them, and watching them play.

In response, this guy paused for a second, looked me square in the eyes, and said, "Well, what the fuck else are you going to do?" He told me about his son, who had graduated from high school the year prior and was now in college. He didn't see him as much anymore and now missed driving him from place to place and watching him play sports. "Your daughter is going to get her driver's license next year. And while I'm sure you're all excited for it since she can drive herself places, you will miss those car rides. Don't wish them away. Cherish them. Make the most of them."

It was a great reminder that the good ol' days are better enjoyed than remembered because we are in them right now. Excellence can only be attained by being present in this moment. Right now. Not by wishing it away or whining and complaining because the hotel sucks and the schedule for the tournament means you'll be in a gym for four full days. Don't wish any of your days away. The present is fleeting. Living in the present is a gift. Give that gift to yourself, your loved ones, and your work each day.

―――――――――― TAKE ACTION ――――――――――

Exercise: Paradox of Success

Why: To keep the main thing the main thing

How: Identify an area of your life in which you are successful. Draw two columns on a piece of paper. In the left column, make a list of the top five actions you took that led to your current success. In the right column, make a list of opportunities your success has provided that could draw you away from your top five actions.

Exercise: Intention and Distraction

Why: To be more intentional

How: Make a list of all the distractions you experience, or could experience, in a single day. Identify at least three you will commit to eliminating today. Explain how this will impact your ability to live intentionally.

CHAPTER 4

The Illusion of Defeat

The world is not driven by greed. It's driven by envy. The fact that everybody is five times better off than they used to be, they take it for granted. All they think about is somebody else having more now. It's built into the nature of things. I have conquered envy in my own life. I don't envy anybody. I don't give a damn what somebody else has. But other people are driven crazy by it.

—Charlie Munger

RH: Every summer since 2009, my younger brother, AJ, has been invited to play in the American Century Celebrity Golf Championship Tournament held at Lake Tahoe. And every summer since 2009, I have gone with him and served as his caddy. It's a really cool event, bringing over eighty celebrities together from across the worlds of professional sports and entertainment to connect and compete in a golf tournament. Getting to spend those four days with AJ each year is an amazing gift I will forever be grateful for.

In 2022, for the final round, AJ was paired to play with Rob Riggle, a twenty-three-year veteran of the United States Marine Corps turned actor and comedian. After joining the USMC as a nineteen-year-old, Riggle served for nine years of active duty in places like Liberia and Afghanistan. While serving in the reserves for fourteen more years, Riggle embarked on his entertainment career, both on television (*Saturday Night Live*, *The Daily Show*, *Modern Family*) and in movies (*The Hangover*, *Talladega Nights*, *21 Jump Street*). Needless to say, he was an interesting person to spend a day with on the links.

As Riggle and AJ talked it up throughout the round, I also got to know the woman serving as Rob's caddy. From the get-go, it was clear that she was right at home on the golf course. Dressed in a custom uniform made to look like she was caddying at the Masters, the woman, who introduced herself as "Kas," exuded expertise as she advised Riggle on proper golf etiquette, helped him align properly off the tee, and shared her read of the greens. After introducing myself and my connection to AJ, I asked Kas how she knew Riggle and what she did for a living. "He's my boyfriend," she said, "and I play golf." Kas, it turns out, was short for Kasia Kay, professional golfer and former contestant on *Holey Moley*, the miniature golf–themed reality game show hosted by Riggle.

After a few holes, I noticed something. As AJ lined up to hit his tee shot, I saw Kas aggressively motioning to get Riggle's attention. Her directive to him was clear: quit watching AJ tee off. Now, that's not the usual practice on any golf course, let alone at an event like this with people who can crush the ball with a driver. My brother murders the golf ball off the tee. His swing is violent. Over the years, AJ has twice won the trophy for the tournament's long-drive competition (and probably would have won more, but they stopped the competition years ago). Of course, with a swing like AJ's, the ball sometimes flies in a direction not exactly in line with where one wants it to go. The sacrifice to accuracy aside, it is golfers like AJ that people enjoy watching off the tee, so Kas's instruction to Riggle got me curious.

As we walked down the fairway after another of AJ's bombs, I said to Kas, "I noticed you telling Rob not to watch AJ tee off. Why is that?"

"As a golfer, you should only be focused on your swing and nobody else's. You want to maintain your tempo," Kas responded. "I don't want Rob trying to match the swing speed of AJ. Rob is older than him, and AJ is a professional athlete. If he watches AJ swing enough times, his body will speed up without him even realizing it. So," she emphasized, "*I want him focused on his swing.*"

"When you play, what do you do while others are swinging?" I asked.

"I look down the fairway or talk with my caddy, but I never watch my fellow competitor's swing," she said. "It's about playing the golf course, knowing your swing, and staying true to it."

It was a great reminder to focus on your work and improve yourself. No comparison to others. Just work on yourself.

THE POISON OF COMPARISON

Avoiding the temptation to compare yourself to others isn't just great advice on the golf course. Any endeavor in which success depends on your performance can be derailed by self-doubt and a comparison to others. This is not the same as the sentiment of "I don't care what anybody thinks" that we often hear people say. People who claim this are either lying to cover for their own insecurities and doubt or are emotionally unwell. It is not only normal but also perfectly healthy to care what *some* people think. The trick is in the who: you should listen to the opinions of the people within your trusted inner circle of care and connection. We get in trouble when we start listening to people outside that circle—which, by the way, is most people. For everyone else, you have to take what they say with a grain of salt or not at all.

Coaching high-school basketball puts Brook in the position of confronting the choice to take or pass on the poison of comparison, especially at a football school in a football town like Centerville, Ohio. "Sending nearly ten players to the National Football League from a single public high school makes you a football school, and rightly so," Brook acknowledges. But ironically, one of the most vivid times of pressure to "drink the poison" came for Brook not at a low point in his coaching career but within the warm afterglow of his greatest coaching accomplishment.

BC: We started the 2020–2021 basketball season just grateful to be playing, given how COVID-19 shut down sports on all levels in the spring and summer of 2020. As a team, we were on the young side, with a starting lineup consisting of two sophomores, two juniors, and one senior. But we knew we had a good team, as they had been playing together since third and fourth grade. Even so, most people assumed our best season would be the following year. The limitations that comparison creates is an aspect of the poison rarely discussed. While we think of comparison as being applied to our current situation, it can also build a wall between what was and what can be. There was talk of league and district championships for our team, but nobody gave any thought to us winning a state championship. Not only had Centerville never accomplished the feat, but the opinion makers had also reserved those title dreams for the large, private schools in Southwest Ohio.

There are several schools in our area that fit that bill. The competition is fierce. But without a doubt, the head of the class is Archbishop Moeller, where the best players in the region go to be a part of its rich athletic and academic tradition and where they receive the benefit of excellent coaching. After winning the state title in 2018, Moeller knocked us out of the state tournament in the Elite Eight in 2019 on the way to its second consecutive state title. In 2020, Moeller did it to us again, ending our season in the Sweet Sixteen just before the remainder of the state tournament was canceled due to COVID-19. But if not for the pandemic, they probably would have won their third consecutive state championship.

The next year, we squared off against Moeller almost right out of the gate, facing them in our third game of the season. If you read the box score of the game, you saw that we lost by thirteen points. If you watched the game play out, you knew the game was not that close. They handled us pretty easily. By the measuring stick of comparison, we didn't stack up. Fortunately, our guys didn't drink the poison.

As the season progressed, our teamwork gelled, and our players' talent shined as a result. By mid-March, we were headed to the regional tournament as the only public school against the likes of Moeller, Elder, and St. Xavier. All three are large, private, all-boys Catholic schools representing the cream of the high-school basketball crop in Ohio. After we earned a hard-fought victory over Elder in the Sweet Sixteen, Moeller awaited us again in the Elite Eight. We were riding a thirteen-game winning streak with a record of 23–3. Our last loss had been in January to the eventual Ohio Division II state champion, St. Vincent-St. Mary.

Our young group had grown so close by this point that the thought of losing did not generate fear. We had accomplished our goal of "attacking opportunities with purpose" day after day. That consistent, season-long approach served them well as we faced Moeller, and once again we were, understandably, underdogs.

The game was tightly played and low scoring; baskets were hard to come by. Although Moeller led for most of the game, we managed to keep it close, never allowing their lead to grow to double digits. With about three minutes remaining in the game, they held a slim lead and began to slow down their play. They spread out into the four corners of the court with the clear goal of holding the ball and milking the clock. Our defense remained focused and patient, waiting for a chance to gather a key rebound or pull off a big steal. Inside the final minute of play, we found ourselves down by just two points and with possession of the ball.

With about twelve seconds left, one of our team's juniors, Tom House, drilled a stone-cold 25-foot three-pointer, giving us the lead. Suddenly, the favorite and two-time defending state champion was desperate. But our defense held strong, and we secured our first regional championship, punching our first ticket to the state tournament.

In the vernacular of our program, we would say, "We didn't flinch." Our guys were not scared, intimidated, or daunted by our opponent's state championship pedigree or even the lopsided score from earlier in the season. It's not that our players weren't aware of them; it's that they didn't compare. Moeller was on their journey, and we were on ours.

The undefeated and top-ranked team in the state awaited us in our semifinal final-four matchup. Once again, our team refused to drink the comparison poison and kept its focus on the only thing we had control of and responsibility for: us. That approach carried us to a double-digit win and the opportunity to play for our school's first-ever basketball state championship.

After a tightly fought battle versus Westerville Central, the final game of our season came down to the final possession of the game. With 2.1 seconds remaining in the fourth quarter, we were clinging to a one-point lead. Our opponent had the ball, out of bounds, under their own basket with a chance to win the game. An entire season's worth of work now came down to defending our goal one last time.

Coming out of the final time-out, our team had recalled our mantra for the season: "Attack every opportunity with purpose." It was something we had established in October and pointed to countless times throughout the year. When everything our guys had worked for was at stake, it again became elevated to the peak of importance. That was the only instruction from the coaches and the single plea from teammates on the bench. I distinctly remember a feeling of calm gratitude prior to the final play—one void of comparison and judgment but full of appreciation and awe. The outcome had been surrendered; we had already won the process.

I wish I could say I felt the same calm gratitude the following season.

With most of our core team returning and coming off a state championship, we were immediately tabbed as the favorite to run away with the title. Throughout the season, the team didn't disappoint, running blemish-free through a schedule pitting us against the best teams not only in Ohio but also from across the country. We were the top-ranked team in Ohio all season and found ourselves as high as number four in the country. The expectations from inside and outside the team grew. The weight of having one of the nation's longest winning streaks grew heavier by the day.

Our guys stayed focused on our goal of "not seeking comfort," but as the wins piled up and the winning streak grew, maintaining this focus became more and more difficult. Despite the growing pressure, we played our best basketball at the end of the regular season. In knocking off a very good prep school from West Virginia in our home gym, we completed the first undefeated regular season in our school's history.

Our march through the postseason looked good on paper. We played well en route to returning to the state-championship game, with some close calls and exciting games along the way. But we were not playing at quite the level at which we had been performing at the end of the regular season. The state championship came down to us and our undefeated winning streak versus Pickerington Central, an extremely talented team from a school with a strong tradition in all athletics. It was the matchup most had predicted when the state tournament had begun.

That game is where our winning streak ended, taking with it our hopes for a second-straight state championship. I don't think we played well, but I've always believed there's a reason teams don't play well. Oftentimes, it's in large part due to the five guys in the other jerseys. Pickerington Central was really good, as were several of our other opponents throughout the year. They played better than we did that day and won. They beat us. That's it.

I had detached from the notion that the result of a single game was the determining factor of my worth as a coach long ago. Likewise, I was not going to allow it to be the lone story of our season-long journey. As these young men traveled through our program, they had heard the importance of the process over the outcome consistently for *years*. To their credit, they had chosen not only to accept but also fully embrace the process we had asked of them.

We put that process to the test thirty times over the course of the season. We were blessed to experience the outcome we'd desired far more than most. We didn't get the outcome we wanted in one of those thirty attempts. In a world that values outcome more than process, the fact that our lone loss came in the season's last game gave it an outsized impact. When we didn't get the desired outcome in one out of thirty attempts, were we supposed to abandon our process? Act as if none of the sacrifice, struggle, and work were worth it? Dismiss the growth and relationships that were created as a result of that process? Prioritize a score on a scoreboard that did not go our way over an entire season of choosing not to seek comfort? All because the 1 in our 29–1 record came at the end of the state tournament in March rather than in the middle of the regular season in December? No way.

But the voices of comparison would answer those questions with a resounding "Yes!" This is the poison of comparison: to value only the results. Comparison is black and white—you either do or you don't. It lifts one by suppressing another. It rewards one by punishing another.

It acclaims and condemns. But more than anything, it marginalizes the single most important aspect of continual growth: the process. How you go about doing things matters. The process is important. And not just for a given situation but also for all that comes after. Comparison demands outcomes and disregards the process. Nothing is more poisonous to excellence than that.

Ignoring the critics was easy; I didn't read anything they wrote. I'm a reflective person, so anything they might have addressed, I had already thought about. Sure, there are things I would have done differently leading up to and during our last game—but that's part of pursuing growth, not comparison. As I looked back at our process and the approach to our program and the season, I felt gratitude and fulfillment. Disappointment in the final result, sure. But I was free from the embarrassment that comparison evokes. Disappointment is an emotion I know will pass. I was proud of the way our guys had approached the game, cared about each other as teammates, and behaved as young men. I was confident and content with the process we had embraced.

THERE IS ONLY GREATNESS

The measure of success is fundamentally found within comparison against others. Often, we use phrases like "winning at life" to talk about living successfully. That is the language of competition, bringing with it the metric of comparison that determines winners and losers. A swimmer who posts a personal-best time in their event has performed well even if she finishes behind other swimmers. In doing so, she "wins" the contest against herself—the game of excellence—even as she loses her competition against others—the game of success.

You can always find somebody who's better at something than you are. Excellence is the pursuit of your personal best by maximizing the gifts you've been given. We want to help people strive for excellence rather than success—to focus solely on becoming the best versions of themselves without the need to compare themselves to their peers.

Sports commentator and former NBA player Kenny Smith said it well on a TNT broadcast for an NBA game: "There's no such thing as the greatest; there's only greatness." This is a countercultural idea because society constantly compares, ranks, and scores. We see success debates everywhere. Could Superman beat the Hulk in a fight? Who is the GOAT (Greatest of All Time) in basketball: Jordan or LeBron? As a quarterback: Montana or Brady? On guitar: Hendrix or Eddie?

Here's the secret to ending these debates: one is not better than the other. They're just different, and both are awesome. Our tendency to keep transactional score means we miss out on appreciating transformational excellence. You can pursue excellence without comparing yourself to anyone else. In fact, it's the optimal way.

TAKE ACTION

Exercise: Attachment Audit

Why: To fight comparison

How: Make two columns on a piece of paper. In the left column, write down the things that are uniquely yours and that you possess. This group is relatively small—your ability to choose your attitude might be one example. In the right column, write down all the things that are not uniquely yours but that you feel like you own and fear losing. This group is likely extensive—your house, your car, your spouse, your reputation, for example.

Note: The fear of losing these things is likely one of the significant sources of pain in your life. Work on changing your mental relationship to one of "borrowing" rather than owning. This will allow you to better appreciate these things while they are present in your life.

Exercise: Compare to Despair

Why: To fight comparison

How: Reflect on these questions:

Where were you five years ago?
    Consider the progress you've made to be where you are.

Who is weighing you down?
    This is usually the people you most often compare yourself to.

Are you creating or consuming?
    When we are in a mindset of creation, we avoid comparison by focusing on new ideas. When we are engulfed in consuming, we see the scarcity of the world rather than the abundance of it.

Who can you lift up today?
    Pointing to others who are shining brightly gives us hope that we can also.

CHAPTER 5

Brick by Brick

No one "builds a house." They lay one brick again and again and again and the end result is a house. A remarkable, glorious achievement is just what a long series of unremarkable, unglorious tasks looks like from far away.

—Tim Urban[1]

Before you can build a house, you have to start by laying a firm foundation. Without one, the structural integrity of the building will be compromised. Not only will it prove fragile in high winds and heavy floods, but also the mere passage of time and the passive weight of gravity will cause the walls to sink, crack, and eventually fall. Even the best-designed building built to the highest manufacturing standards will be laid low without the strength of a solid foundation.

The same is true for anyone who aspires to build a legacy of leadership. No amount of effort toward improvement undertaken with the noblest of intentions can overcome the absence of a solid foundation of personal excellence.

You have to be able to lead yourself before you can lead others. It starts with digging the hole—the personal excavation work of self-reflection. But once that has been done, what you pour into that space matters a lot. Core values that sound nice but aren't really true for you are like cement that never sets. There is no strength there, and it will not stand. We have to know who we are and what we're here for. The more solid your foundation, the higher you can build.

LEVEL 5 MOMENTS

Our lives are a series of moments. Most of the time, we pass from moment to moment with little to no consideration of what just happened. Unfortunate at best, our lack of awareness can rob us of crucial glimpses into the person we are or hope to become. Fortunately, all is not lost because all moments are not created equal. Consider a spectrum from one to five on which the impact of all of our experiences in life fall. The majority of life is lived from one to four, but occasionally we have significant events that shape how we see the world and live within it. These are Level 5 moments. Level 5 moments are special, memorable. An intentional reflection on these specific moments shines a spotlight on what matters to you and your values. After all, there is a reason why we remember these moments over the others.

CORE VALUES

Here's the thing about core values: you have them. Whether or not you know them, acknowledge them, or have ever thought of them, you have them. Everyone operates on a set of standards and beliefs, known or unknown. It's impossible to operate in a vacuum when it comes to values. Even the attempt to value everything or nothing values something by default. Intentionality and direction are necessary for excellence to flourish. We never drift upstream.

So, the issue with core values isn't whether or not you have them. The real question is whether yours are the product of intention. Are they the result of focused thought and directed choice-making?

Many people talk about values. They proudly list several honorable beliefs in their social-media bios but could not begin to tell you what any of them actually mean. Worse, the behaviors we observe from them are often in direct contrast with the very values they claim to hold.

While self-awareness can help you determine your core values, that's just the first step. Having identified them, it takes more thoughtful work to clarify and articulate them with precision. The next piece of the puzzle is to determine the critical actions or behaviors that align with those values. This is arguably the most important step of the process: identifying the behaviors that bring the values to life and making it a daily practice to execute them. Aligning our behaviors with our values is essential to living intentionally. For a team, it's what allows your culture to be authentic. Because your culture is based on *what you do* more than what you say.

One helpful way to discern your core values is to reflect on the three or four most impactful people in your life. Not only will this help you see the values that matter to you most, but it can also be a great way to isolate the behaviors most critically related to those values. Ask yourself: "Who has had the biggest impact in my life? Who do I aspire to be like, and why? What are the actions they've taken that bring their values to life?"

It's important to limit the number of values we aspire to have. If we try to stand for everything, we stand for nothing. It's easy to think that adopting numerous values is better than holding a few, but the opposite is true. It takes more work and intention to be selective about your values than it does to include everything.

Brook's Core Values

Throughout several years of trial and error, I have settled on four personal core values: tough, passionate, unified, and thankful.

Tough comes directly from my dad. He was a teacher and coach for thirty-five years after growing up dirt-poor in a home ruled by an alcoholic father. He and his two brothers attended fifteen different high schools among them, and they often came home to find their dad physically abusing their mom.

As a high-school senior, my dad made the decision to join the US Air Force. He told me years later, "I knew I had to get out of there, or I was going to end up the exact same." His willingness to make such a huge change in the trajectory of his life exemplifies what toughness is all about. That decision changed the course of my life, my brother's life, and both of our families' lives before we were even born.

In the Air Force, my father earned his degree and eventually became a teacher. He was the first in his family to attend—let alone graduate from—college. Not surprisingly, my brother and I both became teachers and coaches. Through his toughness, he rewrote the playbook for not only his life but also ours. His choices have afforded my children the opportunities they have. Given all that he has overcome, he has never been big on complaints or excuses. He is the standard of toughness in my life.

Passionate is critical to the disciplined attitude of persistent work. It flows through me from both my father and my high-school coach, Dave Zeller. My dad was my archetype for a passionate work ethic. When you feel good, you work. When you feel bad, you work. When you play well, you work. When you play poorly, you work. For my dad, it was always about simply doing his job. He never missed work, and he never just cruised through the day putting forth minimal effort. His integrity to his work was never in question.

Coach Zeller exhibited a willingness to go above and beyond what was expected with regard to preparation and service to others in a way that impacted all those around him. Beyond my parents, Coach provided me with a living example that it's what you do outside of the expected that makes the difference. Everything in life is determined by the extra.

Within our team, we talk about choosing extra work in reference to our Breakfast Clubs. These daily six-in-the-morning workouts eventually challenge even the most passionate players. They begin wondering if their daily work is really making a difference. Just as a lumberjack sees little progress in his first ten or twenty swings, the minimal advancement of skills in a single morning workout may seem futile. It's only when you group the consistency of hundreds of swings or months of workouts together that you can truly appreciate the headway extra work yields. Consistent, faithful, and more than what's expected. It's all in the extra.

Unified can really be attributed to all my former teammates and current foxhole friends. I realized a long time ago that I'm not that good alone. I'm not that talented at anything, but within a team, I can contribute my strengths and help others do the same. Within a team, I can be great. When I talk about being unified, I usually reference a wolf. The pack is what makes a wolf great, and the wolf is what makes the pack great. I feel this way about being a part of a team. A united team is one of the most powerful forces on earth.

All leaders want their teams to be whole. We want our families and the teams we lead at work to be whole, and even our social groups are best when they are whole. But we have to work to achieve and maintain this unity. It certainly doesn't just happen by chance. Yet that's exactly how most leaders go about creating a team. We put a bunch of people with different backgrounds, experiences, and perspectives together and then hope for the best. When it doesn't work, we cite the individual struggles each person brought to the table and the gaps their talents left in our team. In reality, it doesn't work because we failed as a leader to unify our group. As Jocko Willink so poignantly pointed out on *The Learning Leader Show*, "There are no bad teams, only bad leaders."[2]

Thankful is a feeling of appreciation, not only for the people in our lives but also for all those who came before us who have allowed us to be where we are now. We've got a quote in our locker room that says, "Drink the water, but remember who dug the well." That's the posture of thoughtful gratitude we aspire to. Few things speak to my heart more than when our current players understand and appreciate the legacy of those who came before them. One of the things we did following our state-championship season was to offer state-championship rings to any alumni of our program. Only a few guys took us up on it, but there were many who reached out and were grateful for the gesture. It provided a great opportunity for the players on that team to understand that they were cutting down nets from the shoulders of those who came before.

Ryan's Core Values

I've gone through this exercise many times over the years. I've struggled to narrow my list down to just four—so much so that in my first iteration, I had twenty core values. I even hung them up on the wall in my kitchen and called them "The Hawk Family Values." But because having twenty priorities is essentially having no priorities, I worked with Brook through a process over the course of many conversations to whittle them down to four. They are thoughtful, thankful, curious, and consistent.

Thoughtful means being intentional with my words and ideas. Being thoughtful comes from my dad's influence on me. Whenever there is a group conversation going on, my dad sits patiently by, taking in what others have to say. Inevitably, someone eventually asks, "Keith, what do you think?" His answer, thoughtfully crafted and expressed in his concise, right-to-the-point style, usually ends whatever debate is going on because he's thought it through and is usually right. It's amazing to have witnessed this for decades. My dad taught me to think before speaking, that you don't need to be the loudest voice in the room or the one doing most of the talking. In fact, you should do the opposite. He encouraged me to be a good listener, to think, and to speak with intention.

I value thoughtfulness also because of the impact that Ron Ullery, my high-school offensive coordinator, had on my life. He showed this by always taking notes—in his office, in meetings, and on the field (both practice and games). I asked him about his note-taking philosophy, and his wife, Lara, sent me a picture of hundreds of 3x5 notecards. He has always documented his thoughts, key learnings, and ideas to improve. This is someone who has been coaching for forty-plus years and remains dedicated to being better each day. His thoughtfulness helps ensure it happens.

When I asked him about this habit, he said, "I'll admit . . . I'm obsessed with being dependable, that other people who count on me know that if I tell them I'm going to do something, they don't have to wonder if I really will do it. My word matters to me. I am always taking notes to ensure I remember an important event, a key learning, or something I want to implement in our program. I take so many notes because I want to be a great teammate to everyone in my life. My notes help me do that."

I've looked up to Coach Ullery since I was fourteen years old. His thoughtfulness has made him an excellent coach, leader, and teammate. I admire that about him and want to be the same. I've adopted a similar note-taking practice to help me document my key learnings to be a dependable teammate for all of the important people in my life.

Thankful as a core value is the product of my parents' influence in my life. My dad always says, "Every day is a holiday; every meal is a banquet." He's so grateful for each day, and his attitude shows it. His gratitude for life brings an energy that always lifts a room. You can tell he's genuinely excited to be where he is with the people he's with, doing what they're doing, regardless of the circumstance. The same quiet behavior I noted in his value of *thoughtfulness* shows up here: he always waits patiently to speak up in a crowd. When we spend Thanksgiving or Christmas with our extended family, my dad listens to everyone intently. He makes others feel heard and, in doing so, shows his gratitude for them and their perspective. My mom's gratitude shines through a more "life of the party" personality. She is always so happy to be with friends and family. She's quick to make a joke, maybe even at your expense (lovingly) to show you that you belong. She's grateful for each day, and it's evident in her exuberance and zest for life. My parents' attitude of gratitude is a key reason they are so often surrounded by friends and loved ones. People love being *with* them.

Curious is best encapsulated in the weird paradox that the more you learn, the more you realize how little you know. Growing up in the greater Dayton area, I've drawn inspiration from curiosity about Dayton's native sons Orville and Wilbur Wright. The brothers who ushered in the age of powered human flight from the workspace of their bicycle repair shop were not intellectual prodigies. They were educated in public schools and grew up, as Orville later explained, in a home where "there was always much encouragement to children to pursue intellectual interests; to investigate whatever aroused curiosity." In a less nourishing environment, Orville believed, "our curiosity might have been nipped long before it could have borne fruit."[3]

I have become more curious over the years after listening to so many people who are far wiser than I on my podcast. Before I interviewed leaders for a living, I thought I knew a lot about being a great leader. After more than five hundred conversations for *The Learning Leader Show*, I realize that I know very little. That fuels my curiosity to learn more.

Consistent is all about showing up every day to do what is necessary, no matter what. My younger brother, AJ, is a great example of this. While in college, he lived by an unwritten rule: no matter what he did the night before, he worked out early in the morning. If he went to a concert and stayed out late with friends, he would still get up the next day to work out. If he won a national championship (which he did as a freshman), the next day he would wake up early and work out. If he lost a game, he would get up and work out. If he won a game, he would get up and work out.

There is a great story about AJ told by one of the Ohio State assistant coaches from his senior season in college. It was very early on the Sunday morning after the Buckeyes had beaten Michigan the day before. The sun had yet to rise as the coach headed into the office to watch film and prepare to meet with his players later in the day. Walking in, the coach passed AJ walking out of the weight room, dripping in sweat. This was the day after AJ had led his team to one of their biggest wins of the year, setting them up for a New Year's bowl game. That game, the last of AJ's college career, was more than a month away. The coach looked at AJ and kept walking to his office. Why? Because that's what he always saw when he came to the office. AJ leaving the weight room in the darkness of predawn meant it was just another day. Nothing about yesterday's win or the long wait before the next game changed that.

Whatever happens, you get up and work. No exceptions. It's easy to work when you feel good. But it's what you do on the days when you aren't feeling 100 percent that makes the difference. AJ still lives by that mantra, and I try to do the same. I love the way New York City mayor Eric Adams said it to me: "I won't beat you with brilliance. I'm going to win with endurance."[4] When you aren't as talented as others, you have to endure. Consistency isn't the sexiest quality, but it's definitely one of the most effective.

———— TAKE ACTION ————

Exercise: Level 5 Moments

Why: To increase self-awareness

How: A Level 5 moment is a time from your past that you clearly remember. Level 5 moments are instrumental in forming your thoughts and beliefs. Identify three for each phase of life: youth (0–10), adolescence (11–20), and adulthood (21+).

Exercise: Core-Value Identification

Why: To create clarity and intention

How: Write down the names of three people you admire. Next to their names, write down what you admire about them. What values do they hold that you aspire to have? Select the six to eight most important values that represent you. Reduce your list to your top three to four.

CHAPTER 6

3 AM Friends

Only gods and heroes can be brave in isolation. A man may call upon courage only one way, in the ranks with his brothers-in-arms . . . A man without a city is not a man.

—Steven Pressfield, *Gates of Fire*

RH: In 2001, researcher Jim Collins published a seminal book on leadership and management titled *Good to Great: Why Some Companies Make the Leap . . . and Others Don't*. He has been one of my leadership heroes ever since I read that book. In 2017, after years' worth of conversations with Collins's team, I got the chance to interview him as a guest on *The Learning Leader Show*.

As we were talking, I excitedly told him what I was doing with my business. I shared how I was doing it and my *why* for doing it. I kept going on and on . . . until he threw up his hands to stop me. "Whoa, slow down for a minute, Ryan. All of those things you're talking about are great, but the single greatest determining factor in your long-term success or failure is your *who*," he said, emphasizing those last two words for effect. "Who will be your mentor? Who will be your friends? Who will be your spouse? Who will you spend your time with? That is what will help you get to where you want to go more than anything else."[1]

I realized at that moment that I had not put a lot of thought into my *who*. Following our conversation, I thought of the people in my life who fit into that important category. As I began jotting down names and thinking about the roles they played in my life, a pattern of organization began to emerge. Instead of just compiling a single list, I discovered, it was more useful to think of these people as having one of three positions in relation to me on the metaphorical road of life: ahead, beside, and behind.

AHEAD

This group represents those who have accomplished what we want to *and* who have done it in a way (with integrity, transformational relationships, leading with trust) we admire. They can be mentors, both formal and informal, but they don't have to be—that is, they don't have to be people you've actually met.

RH: "If you are not inspired, you will not inspire other people." That is what best-selling author Todd Henry told me during one of his appearances on the podcast.[2] His focus was on the *idea inputs* we have in our life. You must take time to read, meet with mentors, and learn from a variety of sources. Pause. Reflect. Just as a diet of healthy food is vital to your long-term health, your content diet is of equal importance. What are you reading each day? What are you watching? Who are you talking to? In other words: Who are the people you are actively learning from?

A few years ago, I realized that watching cable news wasn't helpful. "Breaking news" has become a ubiquitous chyron across the bottom of the screen, regardless of the channel, the time of day, or the topic discussed. Nothing is really "breaking news" if everything is.

Instead of watching the news—most of which will be forgotten a few months from now—I've found it best to direct my content-consuming attention elsewhere. I subscribe to the newsletters sent out by thoughtful writers like Polina Pompliano, Tim Urban, Kat Cole, and Morgan Housel. Their work is a more nourishing meal of information and perspective that helps me view the world from a different lens. I've become a better husband, father, and leader since I stopped watching breaking news and began focusing my attention more on higher-signal, curiosity-inducing content from thoughtful people.

BESIDE

People in this category share a growth-oriented posture with us. We are there for each other when we screw up as well as to celebrate when we do well. We are side by side in a no-judgment zone free of any hidden jealousy or envy when life goes well for the other. Instead, there is genuine excitement for one another when warranted. These are the people we are in meaningful relationships with, be they loving family members or trustworthy friends.

If you think about your core values as a foundation, then the relationships you have with those closest to you can be thought of as the reinforcing steel structure that sets the shape and adds strength to the foundational cement. Often, this role of reinforcement falls by default to our family and the readily available friends and colleagues in our immediate proximity. But all friendships are not created equal. "Foxhole friends" are different. These are people I can absolutely trust who will be completely open with me. They won't hold anything back that

I need to hear and will tell me the truth even if I don't *want* to hear it. They know that I'll do the same for them. They understand that I want to get better, and to help me do that means they may have to be critical sometimes. Writer Adam Grant calls these people "disagreeable givers."[3] They love you enough to be honest.

BC: My foxhole friends are the guys I can call at 3 AM to come pick me up. Even if they live three hours away, they're not going to give me some excuse. They're just going to get up, put their clothes on, and come and get me because I said I needed them to. I know this to be true from experience. Late one weeknight in college, my car broke down a few miles from campus. First, I called my roommate of two years to see if he would pick me up. He was polite but declined, citing an obligation he was heading out the door to attend. The best I got from him was an invitation to call him back if I couldn't find anyone else to help me.

My next call was to one of my friends on the basketball team. He didn't hesitate: "Sure thing, no problem." Not only did he come pick me up, but also, together, we pulled my car to his dad's house, where it sat until I could get it fixed. Those are different relationships. Foxhole friends are the people in your life you can count on, no matter what, regardless of what's going on in their lives. Your relationship is a priority to them.

Choose your foxhole friends carefully. Who do you surround yourself with? Who will you invite into those positions of intimate vulnerability and extreme two-way trust? You become the average of the people you spend the most time with. You begin to take on their character traits *because* you spend so much time together. That's why choosing close friends, your life partner, and others in your inner circle is so important.

Because of this position of deep trust, foxhole friends are that inner group of people whose opinions we value even as we ignore the judgmental noise of the crowd. They help us when we get stuck comparing ourselves to others. They prevent us from listening intently to the poisonous criticism of people who do not have our best interests at heart. They are the people in your foxhole—no matter how deep, dark, cold, and wet it may be—fighting alongside you. They care about you *as a person*.

YOUR SQUAD

Jimmy Donaldson started making videos of himself playing video games and uploading them to YouTube when he was eleven years old. When his first video about an obscure computer game hit twenty thousand views, Jimmy was hooked. Throughout his childhood and teen years, Donaldson had "a hyper obsession" (his words) with becoming a professional YouTuber. His goal was to make enough each month so that, by the time he graduated from high school, he would be able to make it his full-time job. Donaldson devoted all his time, effort, and attention to making this project work, but all he really had to show for it was a transcript full of terrible grades and regular arguments with his mom. "We would fight all the time . . . I never once studied. I literally wouldn't even take my books home. I legit don't think I studied once all of high school at my house." By the time Jimmy had turned eighteen and graduated from high school, he was failing miserably. "I was only making a couple hundred bucks a month," he recalled during his appearance on *The Joe Rogan Experience*.[4] That would change once Jimmy got intentional about his *who*.

He connected with four other guys who shared the same goal but were having little success. Donaldson referred to them as his "four lunatics." "Three of us were college dropouts, one was a high-school dropout, and one [had] just quit his job," Donaldson said. "We were all super-small YouTubers." This group had a simple plan: meet via Skype every day for one thousand days in a row. "We would just call it 'daily mastermind,'" said Donaldson. "Some days I'd get on Skype at 7 AM and I'd be on the call until 10 PM, and then I'd go to bed, and I'd wake up and do it again." Everyone in the group engaged in "hyper study" of the common characteristics of the platform's most viral videos. "What makes a good video? What makes a good thumbnail? What's good pacing?" When the group began its cooperative learning effort, each member had a subscriber count for their respective channels between ten thousand and twenty thousand. At the end of the thousand days, each one of them had channels with subscriber counts in the millions.

Today, Jimmy "Mr. Beast" Donaldson's YouTube enterprise employs over one hundred people, has over 150 million total subscribers, and has raised and donated millions of dollars to charities and nonprofits to help others. He's leaving a big dent in the world, and it started with those daily mastermind talks with others who were on the same journey he was on and were as curious as they were ambitious. Rarely do you see a lone genius create something that impacts millions of people. As Jayson Gaignard, founder of MastermindTalks, said, "We are all community made." Nobody is self-made. It's worth the time and effort to develop relationships with others who will level you up—people who will push you beyond your current zone of comfort and competency and who genuinely want to see you do well (and you for them). That will play as big a role in your long-term impact on others as any other characteristic or quality that you possess.

BC: Although "Mr. Beast" was able to connect with like-minded people within his specific area of interest, the real power of the group was not in the information it possessed. It was in the *mindset* of learning together. That outlook is what we should look for in the people we strive to connect with. The *how* and *why* we do something can be applied to any aspect of our lives we choose. The domain-specific knowledge is far easier to find and teach. The best example of this for me occurred in my first head-coaching position. When I was the basketball coach at

St. Paris Graham High School, I became really good friends with Jeff Jordan, legendary wrestling coach and winner of twenty-two consecutive state championships (along with a pair of national championships). That's a solid résumé for a public high school of about 750 students in the rural farm country of western Ohio.

I did not realize it at the time, but our relationship was the start of my first mastermind group. The sports were different, but the mentality around excellence was the same. Thanks to that relationship, I began looking for other like-minded people to connect with. To this day, Jordan and I are still close friends. I now also count among my close friends a few football and basketball coaches, a cross-country coach, a baseball coach, a pastor, a podcast host, a construction worker, and a guy who runs a branch of a fiber-optics company. The key attributes? They tell the truth, they genuinely embody the "never arriving, always becoming" ethos, and they truly care about me as a person.

A CAVEAT

It is easy to overlook something fundamental when looking within ourselves to identify our core values. This is because those values are all related to a question so basic that many never stop to really think about their answer to it: What do you want?

RH: For instance, curious is a core value for me because I want the growth that comes from being curious about the world around me and, maybe even more, the world *inside* me.

Deciding what you truly want in life seems simple enough, right? Not necessarily.

Luke Burgis is the author of *Wanting* and sat down for a conversation on *The Learning Leader Show*. "Human desire is part of a social process . . . we learn to want things because other people wanted them first."[5] This idea of desire as imitation has a name—"mimetic desire"—and an intellectual source: twentieth-century French social scientist and literary critic René Girard. Desires are not the same as biological needs. When we thirst, our drive to get water arises out of our own instinctual imperative. It is not a desire prone to being directed by the drive to imitate others. But the decision to buy the $2.99 bottle of San Pellegrino water over the $0.99 store-brand bottle of water? That is almost entirely about the cultural markers at play in mimetic desire.

RH: Early in my career, I had a colleague who had just earned his first promotion to become a manager. A few weeks later, he walked over to a group of us and said, "Come outside. I want to show you something." Out in a sea of Honda Civics and old Toyota Corollas was a brand-new, candy-apple-red Corvette.

"Check out my new ride," he said. "I thought I'd treat myself after getting promoted." We all kind of looked at each other.

"Oh, wow. Cool car, man. Did you grow up loving Corvettes?"

"No, I just thought it would look sweet to be driving one."

He wasn't a car guy. He didn't have a fan's appreciation of the engineering under the hood or the artistry of its design. He wanted a Corvette because he thought he would look cool.

As writer Morgan Housel told me during his appearance on *The Learning Leader Show*, "I wrote a letter to my son after he was born, and it said, 'You might think you want an expensive car, a flashy watch, and a huge house. But you don't. What you want is respect and admiration from other people, and you think having expensive stuff will bring it. It almost never does. Especially from the people you want to respect and admire you.'"[6] What Housel understood that my former colleague did not was the false promise of mimetic desires.

Mimetic desire happens in all aspects of our lives if we aren't intentional about creating and living our values. Left unexamined, mimetic desire can take over even the best of intentions when it comes to designing our lives around purpose, accomplishment, and impact. A lot of us don't do the reflection to actually know what our purpose is, to know what lights us up, to know what we actually want. Or, if we do take the time, we go through the motions of self-awareness without really digging down to figure out not just *what* we want in life but also *why* we want it. We spend too much time focused on the wrong scoreboard—mimetic imitation and external validation—and not enough on what really matters. This is the natural current of our cultural evolution as a social species. It takes focused, intentional effort to swim upstream against that current to identify the purpose, goals, and values that are truly your own.

BEHIND

The people in this final category are those who are not as far along in their journey and whom we can help. There are two reasons to focus on those who aren't quite at our level yet. One, it's the right thing to do. We should always look for ways to help others. Two, teaching someone else is one of the greatest tools for your own learning.

Consider what the *New York Times* has referred to as the "Shalane Effect." At the 2000 Summer Olympics in Sydney, Australia, only one American woman qualified to participate in the marathon. Her name was Dr. Christine Clark, a thirty-seven-year-old pathologist and mother. Her victory at the US Olympic trial event was a surprise for more reasons than one. Her training regimen consisted of running 30–40 *fewer* miles than the average, two-thirds of which were on an indoor treadmill during the long winter in her home in Anchorage, Alaska. And yet, Clark's time was more than seven minutes faster than her personal best, despite having to run in the heat of South Carolina, where the February temperature peaked at above eighty degrees. But because the winning team was "slower than the Olympic 'A' qualifying standard," only the winner would be certified by USA Track & Field to represent the United States at the Olympics.[7] In Sydney, Clark finished nineteenth out of fifty-three runners, despite posting another new personal best time.

Training to become an Olympic marathoner was a lonely, isolated, and highly competitive endeavor. "After college," wrote journalist Lindsay Crouse, "promising female distance athletes would generally embark on aggressive training until they broke down. Few of them developed the staying power required to dominate the global stage. And they didn't have much of a community to support them; domestic women's distance running was fractious and atrophied."[8]

And the results were proving to be more miss than hit by the time a woman named Shalane Flanagan first entered the scene of professional long-distance running a few years later. After graduating from the University of North Carolina at Chapel Hill as a two-time national champion—twice named as the best female collegiate cross-country runner—Flanagan applied her maniacal work ethic and intense dedication as a professional. She did very well, earning a silver medal in the 10,000 meters at the 2008 Olympics in Beijing.[9]

But Flanagan had bigger intentions. In 2009, she joined a running group in Portland, Oregon, called the Bowerman Track Club. At the time she joined, she was the lone woman in the group. Not only did she want to begin competing in marathon and half-marathon events, but she also wanted to "create something new: a team of professional female distance runners who would train together and push one another to striking collective success." Before long, Flanagan and the women training with her began to outperform the men in the club. Instead of the women being threatened by one another's success, they embraced each other. Flanagan brought in even more women and elevated the group further.[10]

According to Lauren Fleshman, herself a championship distance runner and author of *Good for a Girl: My Life Running in a Man's World*, Flanagan "pioneered a new brand of 'team mom' to these young up-and-comers, with the confidence not to tear others down to protect her place in the hierarchy . . . [Her] legacy is in her role modeling, which women in every industry would like to see more of."[11] "I thoroughly enjoy working with other women," Flanagan reported to the *New York Times*. "I think it makes me a better athlete and person. It allows me to have more passion toward my training and racing. When we achieve great things on our own, it doesn't feel as special."[12]

What happened as a result of Flanagan's approach to building her team of women to help push each other to run at their maximum level? All eleven of her training partners qualified for the Olympics. But it didn't just benefit those who followed Flanagan's lead. It boosted her own performance as well: in 2017, she became the first American woman to win the New York City Marathon since 1977.

Your *who* is everything. The research and practice are clear. The people with whom you surround yourself shape you. They have a massive impact on your motivation, performance, and well-being. Choose wisely.

--------- TAKE ACTION ---------

Exercise: Foxhole Teammates

Why: To identify your inner circle

How: Draw a circle on a piece of paper. Think of a clock. You are facing 12:00. Write the name of the person you trust the most at 6:00. Write the names of the next two most trustworthy people at 3:00 and 9:00. This is your foxhole. Send these people an email, text, or letter letting them know they are in your foxhole and how important they are to you.

Exercise: Board of Directors

Why: To identify your mentors

How: Draw a line horizontally in the middle of a piece of paper. Write your name on that line. Draw five horizontal lines above your name. Write the names of five people who could provide you with guidance and direction. They should not only have experienced what you want to but should also embody how you want to do it. Send them an email, text, or letter letting them know how important they are to you.

CHAPTER 7

Your Critical Behaviors

The objective is not to learn to mimic greatness, but to calibrate our internal meter for greatness. So we can better make the thousands of choices that might ultimately lead to our own great work.

—Rick Rubin, *The Creative Act: A Way of Being*

When it comes to assessing what a person or organization values, nothing is more telling than the behaviors they choose to adopt. Many are the corporate office walls and website "Who We Are" pages emblazoned with artistic renderings of high-sounding mission statements, lists of company values, and other finely tuned words aimed at inspiring employees and customers alike. And yet, all too often, neither the company's behaviors nor the customers' experiences match up with these lofty pronouncements.

CRITICAL BEHAVIORS

In order to take your core values beyond words on a page and make them real, the first step is to identify the behaviors that help you live them. As with your values, the goal isn't quantity but quality. This should not be an exhaustive list of everything one can or should do in the name of the value of *gratitude*, for example. Rather, as with the core values themselves, the goal is to identify a behavioral action step that, when taken, leads you in the direction of the fixed compass heading of your core value.

BC: I want to be intentional about living my values, and the behaviors are the crux. It took me a long time and a lot of conversations with people I trust to figure these out.

Tough: Positive Body Language

To me, toughness means maintaining a posture of being ready to attack opportunities regardless of the circumstances swirling around me, whether on or off the court. In our basketball program, failing to maintain positive body language is a cardinal sin. We are emphatic about not allowing players to pout, put their head down, throw their hands up at officials, slouch in meetings, or saunter into practice. Our consistent emphasis on maintaining positive body language colors everything we do, whether we're dealing with morning workouts, weightlifting sessions, off-season conditioning, adversity in games, failure in the classroom, mistakes with friends, and issues at home. We want to help our players be tough in all aspects of their lives, and that begins with a positive mindset expressed through our body language.

Passionate: Choosing Extra Work

There are many behaviors that could serve as evidence of passion. I look for people who are consistently choosing extra work. The willingness to embrace even mundane work is closely tied to the belief that we are "always becoming." We will never come to a point at which the basics are not important. In that vein, I'm reminded of a quick conversation with my son, Gabe, early in his basketball career. By fourth grade, he was already committed to practicing two or three times per day. Once, he asked me if he should still work out that day, given that he had a game. I replied by asking if he would have any more games after the one that day. "Well, yeah," he confirmed quickly. "Do you want to be better for those games?" I asked. "Well, yeah," he confirmed again. "So, what do you think?" I offered. "I want to work out," he said.

You see, it's the idea that a game, a presentation, or an interview is some type of final event that justifies our bringing an end to a process. But these things are rarely final, singular events. They are part of an ongoing tapestry of interconnected events. The work to prepare for them is no different. We mistakenly think we are preparing for a singular event when we are actually training behaviors that will produce fruitful experiences throughout our lives. Gabe has carried out that game-day workout decision he made as a ten-year-old ever since. In the last three years of high school, that equates to about 240 hours of additional practice, or ten full days of practice. He now has a mindset that embraces stealing inches, or consistently doing the little things most choose not to do. Jeff Olson said it well in his book *The Slight Edge: Secret to a Successful Life*: "The truth is, what you do matters. What you do today matters. What you do every day matters. Successful people just do the things that seem to make no difference in the act of doing them and they do them over and over until the compound effect kicks in." An inch here and there isn't a big deal, but an inch every day for ten years . . . now *that's* a big deal.

Unified: Speaking and Acting with Urgency

At first, people may ask, "What does speaking and acting with urgency have to do with being united?" The urgency here is in the context of holding each other accountable for anything that isn't oriented in the direction of team success. If you are choosing to remain quiet when someone is doing something that's detrimental to the team, you are choosing your personal comfort over the good of the team. That's self-ish, and that's the opposite of united.

This is a major concept in our program. We want a player-led team, not a coach-led team. Speaking and acting with urgency is critical to that distinction. It's not natural for grown adults, let alone kids, to do the kind of accountability work necessary to keep a team united and focused. Teaching young folks how to do it and getting them comfortable doing it is a process that starts with trust. Patrick Lencioni's vulnerability-based trust is really where we start: we have to know each other before we can really trust each other. We spend a lot of time breaking down walls and creating vulnerability among team members. Getting guys to open up, share vulnerabilities, and tell stories in the locker room is a big deal. Players will laugh, cry, hug, and say "I love you" more than you can imagine. It's not easy to get there, but the camaraderie is tangible and something players miss more than any game they played or championship they won. Eventually, that all goes back to accountability: being willing to hold the other person accountable. Speaking and acting with urgency are signals that united teams possess, regardless of the field.

We've certainly failed at doing this from time to time with teams we've led. In reflection, we can see how the failure flowed from one thing: a lack of courage. We know what needs to be done for a team to be at its best; we all do. But knowing isn't doing. We get what we allow in leadership, and that axiom certainly holds true when it comes to being united. The speaking and acting parts of the behavior are critical, but it's the urgency piece that is most often missing. The issue isn't about knowing what should be done or having the actual ability to point it out; the issue is saying or doing it *now* without flinching.

Thankful: Showing Love

We express gratitude through acts of love. This value is definitely a byproduct of the love my mom shares. It's not just for me, though I know she loves me as her son. Her love is for life and experiences together. She never thinks of herself first, and she is always looking for ways to serve others. She is the most selfless person I've ever met. I hope to continue growing to appreciate and be grateful for all aspects of life as she does. I'm still aspiring to be more like my mom.

Love is impossible to measure, but showing love is easy to see. Kind words, asking about a family member, giving a car ride, saying "happy birthday," bringing someone their favorite snack—the list is endless. The challenge, of course, is that a mindset of gratitude must precede any action of gratitude. It's this heart posture my mom has that I strive for.

RH: When it comes to implementing my core values in my daily life, these are the critical behaviors by which I judge how well I'm *living* my values.

Thoughtful: Seeking to Understand

This stems from habit number five of Stephen Covey's *The 7 Habits of Highly Effective People*: "Seek first to understand, then to be understood." To me, being thoughtful means always trying to understand the perspective and point of view of the other person prior to sharing my views with them. If we have differing opinions, I stop to consider why that is. Maybe they're right. Maybe I'm wrong. Being thoughtful means having an open mind. The old adage is true: Your mind is like a parachute. It only works when it's open.

Thankful: Leaving It Better

I am grateful for the generous environment I have lived in. I was born in America to two amazing parents and an older and younger brother who all love and support me. We never wanted for anything. My parents love each other and are the ultimate models for having a great family. Because of all that amazing luck, I feel a responsibility to leave people, places, and things better than I found them. The way I show gratitude for the good fortune I've had is to do whatever I can to make things a little better for everyone around me. So, it's a conscious thought with each interaction: *What can I do to leave that person in a better place than they were in when they met me? How can I help them? Are they in pain? Do they need a job? An introduction?*

Curious: Stretching My Zone of Competency

One prompt I ask myself at the end of the day is "What did I do to push my edges today?" Pushing my edges means doing something challenging and outside of my comfort zone. By having regular conversations with people who are wiser than me (which I do for my podcast every week), I am stretching my current zone of competency. The work I put in to prepare for each conversation, talking with the person who has specific expertise, and then writing the show notes that translate that conversation for readers who may not have heard it—all of that stretches me big time. I grow from each step in the process.

Consistent: Showing Up

This is core to everything I do. I'm not particularly brilliant at anything. However, I am willing to endure. My ability to show up each day, regardless of how I feel, is what will make the difference. It's not that hard to show up every once in a while, to work hard sometimes, to be in the gym on the first day when we're all excited. What's hard is to consistently show up day after day no matter what. Occasionally saying yes to your daughter when she asks you to play soccer or volleyball in the backyard is easy. Doing it *every time* is more challenging. Kids don't care if you're tired from a long day at work. They care about being with you while doing something they enjoy. The answer is always *yes*. No matter what.

SAYING NO

Our critical behaviors are the means by which we live our core values, so it's what we focus on, but we also express our core values by what we say no to.

Among the various definitions of the word *focus* are "a center of activity, attraction, or attention" and "to concentrate attention or effort."[1] Picture looking through a telescope at the craters on the moon. You use the sighting scope to focus the telescope's lens at the feature you want to see, and then you adjust the knobs to bring it into clearer view. Focus entails both knowing what you want to focus on and putting in the work to aim your attention accordingly.

But notice something. As you look through the telescope, most of your field of vision is filled with black nothingness. The focusing effect of the telescope does more than just enhance the cold white beauty of the lunar moonscape. It also blocks out everything else. To be focused on something means turning your attention away from all the rest.

"People think focus means saying yes to the thing you've got to focus on," Steve Jobs said from the stage of the Worldwide Developer Conference in 1997. "But that's not what it means at all. It means saying no to the hundred other good ideas that there are. You have to pick carefully. I'm actually as proud of the things we haven't done as the things we have done. Innovation is saying no to one thousand things."[2]

It's one of the most enduring attributes that people who worked closely with Jobs took away from the experience. Jony Ive was the creative-design force behind most of Apple's most iconic products, from the first iMac to the history-changing iPhone and the tech-turned-fashion-statement Apple Watch. "What focus means," Ive told an audience for *Vanity Fair*, "is saying no to something that, with every bone in your body, you think is a phenomenal idea, and you wake up thinking about it, but you say no to it because you're focusing on something else."

RH: Over the course of these last nine years doing my podcast, I have had the pleasure of having Ryan Holiday as a guest seven times. Holiday is a prolific writer, having published a book a year for a decade. Most of them are international bestsellers. That is an incredible pace of producing high-quality work. Writing even one great book requires an immense amount of focus. On one of his latest appearances on *The Learning Leader Show*, I asked him how he stays focused on his work. He said, "Right behind my computer, I have a picture of my youngest

[son] and a picture of my oldest [son]. In between those pictures, I have a sign that simply says 'No'—which to me is a constant reminder that when I say *yes* to additional work, additional hours, or new speaking gigs, I'm saying no to other things in my life. Often, those things are my family or my free time. Sacrifices have to be made."[3]

This idea of sacrificing things according to their priority is at the center of minimalist thinking. Intentional living, as it turns out, is really about eliminating the nonessentials in your life. Getting rid of what does not matter is about more than decluttering our living spaces of excess stuff. It is also about pruning the dead wood from our mind and from our actions.

From a coaching and athletic perspective, we see examples of this all the time. What do teams, coaches, and players do when they are in a performance funk or have lost a few games in a row? They get back to the fundamentals. A basketball shooter spends extra time after practice taking shot after shot after shot. A baseball player in a hitting slump takes extra time in the batting cage. What people on the path to excellence realize is that the time to focus on the fundamentals never passes. It's always time. The main thing is always the main thing, and they focus their efforts on keeping it that way.

It's important to note that both failure and success pull us from a focus on the main thing. After significant failure, we will do pretty much anything to taste success. We will compromise standards and values and try anything we think might lead to a win. However, success can have a very similar effect on us. Greg McKeown, author of *Essentialism*, refers to it as the paradox of success. On *The Learning Leader Show*, he said, "Success can distract us from focusing on the essential things that produced success in the first place. More opportunities [and] options lead to diffused efforts."[4] In short, we stop keeping the main thing the main thing.

─────────── TAKE ACTION ───────────

Exercise: Critical-Behavior Discovery

Why: To live your values through action

How: Consider each core value you've identified. What do the people you admire do? What do they *not* do? What actions do they take that tell you they hold the core value you admire? Select a single behavior for each core value that is applicable in all aspects of your life. Commit to memory your critical behavior for each core value.

Exercise: No Excuses

Why: To increase ownership

How: Write down three instances in the last two weeks when you made an excuse. How do you feel about that decision now? Write down three instances in the last two weeks when you had the opportunity to make an excuse but chose not to. How do you feel about those decisions now?

CHAPTER 8

Hawks and Wolves

Excellence is not a fixed standard that applies to everyone. It's a personal quest that reflects your values, passions, and aspirations. Don't compare yourself to others or chase external validation. Define excellence for yourself and pursue it with integrity.

—Steve Magness

Wolf. Axe. Arena. What do you think of when you read those words?

How about *hawk*, *edge*, and *stairs*?

These are the words and symbols we use to express our values within the context of a story. They form our ethos. An ethos is "the characteristic spirit of a culture, era, or community as manifested in its beliefs and aspirations."[1] It's who you are. Your ethos is the culmination of all your experiences and the beliefs you've developed as a result of them. The imagery is important. You want your ethos to be communicated through the images you select. They are the images you sink into your foundation as you lay it, and they guide your actions every day.

We are well versed in identifying the ethos of others. Within a few interactions, we have a good idea what others believe and what they aspire to do. Their actions tell us all we need to know. The same is true for us. Our *true* ethos is that which our actions demonstrate. Excellence happens when we close the gap between the two: when the ethos of our actions aligns with the ethos of our ideals.

To better illustrate this, we want to share the imagery that we each hold along with how it relates to our aspirational core values (ideals) and our critical behaviors (actions).

BC: My values of *tough, passionate, unified, and thankful* are the fountain from which my ethos flows. My imagery consists of a wolf, an axe, and an arena.

THE WOLF

When I think of toughness, I think of the wolf. I love this quote: "Lions and tigers are cool, but you won't find a wolf in the circus." Lions and tigers can be subdued and trained to jump through hoops and live in a cage. Not the wolf. I relate to that because I've never been the lion, the strongest or most powerful. Neither have I been the tiger, which is always portrayed as a smooth operator.

In his poem "The Law of the Jungle," Rudyard Kipling wrote, "For the strength of the Pack is the Wolf, and the strength of the Wolf is the Pack."[2] This, as much as because of the wolf's wild spirit, is why I identify so much with this image. It encapsulates what it means to be united. I'm better with a team around me. I have always been at my best as a member of a pack. I feel like I can elevate a team and be elevated by it in turn. In doing so, I can accomplish far more than if I were working on my own.

THE AXE

The axe represents work, but not the work we want to do or the work we're expected to do. The axe symbolizes consistent, faithful work—extra work that surpasses the standard and establishes a level of excellence. Often, that work is harder and takes longer than we first imagine. We always underestimate what excellence is going to require.

Our yearly activity of chopping down a tree reinforces this concept. Before our team members start, we ask them how many swings they think it's going to take. The guesses they throw out always end up being far fewer than what it actually takes, strengthening the mindset to "keep chopping."

THE ARENA

The arena touches on a few different aspects of the value of being thankful. First is the concept of comparison. If you pursue excellence with any amount of seriousness, you will inevitably encounter other people's opinions of what you're doing, which can be discouraging if you let it. The image of the arena comes from part of a speech titled "Citizenship in a Republic," delivered by Theodore Roosevelt in Paris on April 23, 1910, a couple of years after his presidency. You've probably come across his "man in the arena" quote before, but just in case you haven't:

It is not the critic who counts; not the man who points out how the strong man stumbles, or where the doer of deeds could have done them better. The credit belongs to the man who is actually in the arena, whose face is marred by dust and sweat and blood; who strives valiantly; who errs, who comes short again and again, because there is no effort without error and shortcoming; but who does actually strive to do the deeds; who knows the great enthusiasms, the great devotions; who spends himself in a worthy cause; who at the best knows in the end the triumph of high achievement, and who at the worst, if he fails, at least fails while daring greatly, so that his place shall never be with those cold and timid souls who neither know victory nor defeat.[3]

If you're not in the arena with me fighting the same fight, I don't feel the need to value your opinion. It's not that I don't like you; it's that I don't care what you think regarding my particular situation. I reserve that influence strictly for those in my foxhole sharing the arena with me.

Second, the arena represents love's conquest over fear. In Roosevelt's passage, fear is the real culprit. The fear of coming up short and being judged is what holds so many of us back. I choose to be grateful for the opportunity to be in the arena, to be with others who share my passion, and to give the best of what I have to offer to whatever endeavor is in front of me. The arena reminds me to choose love over fear.

Lastly, the arena is about surrendering. Being grateful for opportunity requires releasing the perception of control, giving your best effort regardless of the situation, and just going for it. This is love in action, free to accept what is. The arena is about laying down your ego and embracing the moment. It's about trusting the process and surrendering the outcome.

RH: My values are *thoughtful, thankful, curious, and consistent.* The symbols of my ethos—the hawk, the edge, and the stairs—illustrate the standards I set for myself.

THE HAWK

The hawk illustrates my dedication to being thoughtful and curious. Hawks are among the most intelligent species of bird on earth, according to Dr. Louis Lefebvre, professor of biology and animal behavior at McGill University in Montréal, Canada. By combing through the more than two thousand "short notes" of unusual bird-behavior sightings noted by the world's birdwatchers in ornithology journals since 1930, Lefebvre built the world's first comprehensive scale of aviary intelligence based on the amount of innovation birds display in their feeding behaviors.[4] His IQ scale is based on a definition of intelligence displayed in the proven propensity for learning and innovation.[5]

The hawk can soar through the air for four to five hours at a time, conserving its energy for use when the time is right. It circles its prey while waiting for the best time to strike. The hawk uses the strength of its eyesight (which is eight times stronger than that of humans) to identify an opportunity (food) and then aggressively pursue it. When the hawk chooses to go, it goes hard and attacks fast. I identify with the ability to be observant and curious and then, when it's time to go, committing to an opportunity with maximum effort.

THE EDGE

Living "on the edge" is a phrase often associated with the excitement of adrenaline-fueled thrill seeking. That's not what I mean here. For me, the image of living at the edge brings to life my value of consistently pushing past my edges of comfort to take the next step of growth.

Jay Hennessey, a twenty-six-year veteran of the Navy SEALs, told me about the kind of work he did toward the end of his time with the military. He was part of the Navy SEAL officer-selection team, and he said he looked for people who were willing to "push their edges."

Because nobody cares what you could do yesterday; they care about what you can do right now, and the only way to get good at that is to always be pushing your edges. To me, this represents the value of growth and challenging myself. What am I going to do today to be wiser when I go to bed than when I woke up? What am I going to do today to make my body physically stronger? My mind tougher? These prompts help me consistently push my edges.

In early 2023, I delivered a keynote speech at a conference in Las Vegas for five hundred soccer coaches from across the country. After my work was done, Miranda and I made the two-and-a-half-hour drive north to Zion National Park. Our plan was to hike as much as we could in two days. On our last hike before heading to the airport, we walked the West Rim Trail. This breathtakingly beautiful trail includes a stretch with seventeen switchbacks up the side of a steep mountain. As it was early February, some of the narrow passageways up the mountain were completely iced over.

As we attempted to hike up the switchbacks, we kept slipping. Slipping over the edge meant falling off a very tall mountain, so this was much more than theoretical danger. Multiple groups of people ahead of us yelled down, "It's way too icy up here, man. You can only do this if you have spikes." We didn't have spikes. A woman ahead of us who had poles and spikes said, "I've been slipping the whole time, and I have spikes. You should turn back; it's too dangerous."

Miranda and I both looked at each other and said, "Well, we've made it up a few of them. Let's see if we can do the next one." And when we made it up that one, "How about one more?" One more? One more. We found that the only way to get enough traction on the ice and to safely get up the mountain was to crawl on our hands and knees. As we encountered others with poles in hand and spikes on their boots who were better prepared for their winter hiking expedition in Zion, they all shared a look that said, "What are those idiots doing?"

Did we look like fools? Probably. Was it embarrassing? To some, it surely would be. But our desire to get to the top of the mountain exceeded our fear of looking stupid to random strangers on a mountain in Utah. Was there a part of us that was quietly motivated by the scores of people saying, "It's not possible without spikes"? No doubt. Was it a stupid thing to do, knowing that we are responsible for children? Maybe. But that's why we crawled.

Miranda said, "Even the people with spikes should crawl. It feels like they are embarrassed to look stupid." If so, they were putting themselves at greater risk out of pride. It's amazing what we will go through to not look stupid. The whole situation reminds me of something my friend Lance Salyers once said about leading: "Find the safest way to do the boldest thing rather than the boldest way to do the safest thing." Sometimes, you have to get on your hands and knees and crawl up the mountain to get to the top . . . which we eventually did. It took a while, but we got there.

The descent down the mountain was also dangerous, especially if we had chosen to stay upright and walk. So, what did we do? We got low to the ground, at times sliding down on our butts, so we could use our hands to create friction and slow ourselves when we got close to the edge. Despite odd looks from confused hikers climbing up with their poles and spikes, we safely made it up and down the mountain and had some fun along the way.

Think of how often you worry about looking stupid or making a fool of yourself and how that puts you in danger or causes you not to make the bold choice. After over five hundred interviews, I've learned that a commonality among leaders who have sustained excellence is the willingness to be a beginner: a lack of fear of looking stupid and the ability to be embarrassed and keep going.

THE STAIRS

The symbol of stairs illustrates my value of being thankful. I am grateful to have a healthy and able body, and because of that, I will do everything within my power not only to maintain it but also to try to improve it each day. One way to do so is by taking the stairs.

The stairs remind me to be a "2 percenter." During a podcast conversation with Michael Easter, author of *The Comfort Crisis*, I learned that we are wired for laziness. When hunting and gathering was the name of the game for Homo sapiens, energy in the form of food was expensive in terms of the time and effort required to obtain it. This meant that energy conservation was an important survival skill. Early humans needed to be energy efficient whenever possible for the hunt or to run away from another predator intent on killing them. Modern man doesn't exist in that same environment, but the changes to that environment have occurred far more quickly than our brains can evolve. So even though we are no longer holding onto life by the amount of physical energy we can bring to a foot chase, we are still driven to conserve energy by finding the easiest way to do everything. In short, we are wired to be lazy, and it takes a conscious effort to deviate from that tendency.

Michael told me about a study where researchers tracked the movements of people at an airport. They camped out at places where travelers could choose between taking the escalator or the stairs. Of the thousands they observed, 98 percent took the escalator. I'd rather take empty stairs than stand still on a crowded escalator. If you have two working legs, take the stairs. Don't take the tram between terminals at the airport; walk from one gate to the next. Be known as someone who doesn't take the easy path. The hard path prepares us for the inevitable adversity we will face in the future.

As the Stoic philosopher Seneca said, "Constant misfortune brings this one blessing: to whom it always assails, it eventually fortifies." Fighting through even small, seemingly insignificant adversity can have a big impact over time. In his book *The Secret Wisdom of Nature*, Peter Wohlleben describes the growth process of trees in a mature, wild forest. In these environments, new saplings take root where they fall as an acorn, a pine cone, or a nut. As a result, they must grow "patiently in their mother's shade." While this may sound positively nurturing, in reality, it means the roots of the young tree have to compete with the far more developed root systems of the surrounding adults for the vital nutrients of sunlight, water, and soil. "As they struggle to put on a few feet," writes Wohlleben, "they develop wood that is incredibly dense."

In contrast, the new trees taking root in the open spaces of managed forests don't face the same obstacles to growing. Without competition, seedlings are free to grow as fast as their cells can process the unobstructed sunlight above and the abundant nutrients below. This rapid growth results in larger growth rings and wood cells that contain more air than normal. This makes these young trees taller more quickly but far more susceptible to the fungi that thrive on the air in more porous wood. A tree that doesn't have to struggle to survive "grows quickly [but also] rots quickly and therefore never has a chance to grow old."

People who grow free from struggle run the same risk. Yes, the stairs are harder. They may even take longer. Choosing the option that is harder and takes more time cuts against the grain of our modern life, which is designed to be easy. Leaders who handle the tough moments well are more impactful than those who do not. They are able to do this because they prepare for those moments every day. Each decision they make to do hard things helps them prepare to do even harder things in the future. It normalizes the hard. Choosing the stairs is one small choice I make to be better prepared for the future. Confidence is built by proving to yourself that you can do hard things . . . and then doing them over and over again.

MANTRAS

Mantras are simple statements repeated frequently. The power of mantras lies in their simplicity. They restore hope when the present appears bleak. They deliver confidence when history questions our worth. They provide direction when we feel lost. They serve as a reminder of the person we aspire to be—a reset button for our core values.

Mantras are a key piece of what coaching consultant and author Brett Ledbetter calls a Failure Recovery System. These are oral and physical rituals that return our focus to the task before us in the present. They are a reminder to quit focusing on the mistake that just happened (now in the past) or on the fear of failing in the next moment of opportunity (still in the future). Results come from the actions taken in the present, which is the only place where we can actively become the person we aspire to be. Combining a simple physical gesture (like the rubbing of one's hands together or the tapping of a green dot) with the verbal act of saying a mantra out loud serves as the perfect framework for an effective Failure Recovery System.

In a lot of ways, our mantras are the most important aspects of our plan for a life of excellence because they bring us back to the people we want to be. They return our mindset to the values we desire to live out. Without a mantra and the awareness of when it is needed, we are like a leaf floating at the mercy of the wind.

In moments of adversity, we choose character or compromise. Character is reverting to our mantra and our values. Compromise is deferring to chance.

It's not a matter of *if* plans will be disrupted but *when*. Things will go wrong. Whether you have a presentation to a potential client, a game plan against a great team, or a long-anticipated family vacation, the surest bet is that things will not go exactly as planned. No amount of self-reflection, purpose discovery, core-value introspection, or behavior identification will allow you to bypass the challenge of adversity staring you in the face.

Life—especially one lived in pursuit of excellence—does not come with guardrails. Excellence requires far too much travel off well-worn, safely paved roads for that. With that in mind, we are best served to establish our own bumpers to ensure we never veer too far from the narrow path of excellence.

Brook's Mantras

> **CORE VALUE |** Tough
> **MANTRA |** "Fight ready."

Having positive body language is our proof that we are "fight ready" no matter what. Think of a boxer entering the ring. I haven't seen too many boxers going into the ring with poor body language. If you're going into a fight, you're going in with a bounce to your step and a mentality that you are attacking whatever is in front of you—or you're not fighting for very long.

Coming prepared to class, leaning forward during meetings, having shoes tied on time, reading and following the scouting report, and getting under the bar in the squat rack with an assertive mentality and posture are all examples of being "fight ready." It's a mentality we expect our guys to embrace rather than any single action we want them to take.

> **CORE VALUE |** Passionate
> **MANTRA |** "Steal inches."

Inches lead nowhere until you realize that, together, they provide the only path to anywhere. In basketball, it's common to see warm-ups in which teams simply divide into two lines and shoot layups. For twenty minutes, each player chooses his own shot at his own speed to prepare for the game. We choose a different path. Our twenty-minute pregame program consists of focused repetition of very specific and critical foundational skills for our team. We pivot. We cut and finish at game speed. We throw clean, sharp passes. We shoot shots we will be shooting in the game. We communicate with purpose. For any single game, this approach doesn't seem like it could deliver any kind of advantage. But over the course of thirty games in a season, those pregame reps add up to a full six additional hours of work on the fundamentals. That is stealing inches.

CORE VALUE | Unified
MANTRA | "Don't flinch."

Maintaining a standard is hard. Giving even one concession against the grain of our core values makes it that much harder to hold the line next time. When it comes to being unified, even the slightest breach in our values can compromise our togetherness. Being an active, engaged member of a team requires making sacrifices not necessary when operating on your own. And, while your own path may be appealing at times, it can never offer the fulfillment that a team can. However, in order to maximize your team, you must have the courage to speak up and uphold the standards necessary to perform at your best. This requires courage.

In today's world, it is common to see athletes wearing any number of headbands, arm sleeves, leg sleeves, or other accessory additions to their uniform. "Look good, play good" is the mindset, but behind it is a desire to stand out, express their individuality, and look different from their teammates. To be sure, there is nothing wrong with individuality and being different. Far from it. But within the context of a team, the impulse to stand out from one's teammates pulls in a direction opposite to being united with them.

Being unified goes beyond teamwork or working together. While those are certainly an aspect of it, they don't quite reach the depth of commitment we desire. To be unified is to be "made one." We want to be one. Accordingly, players in our basketball program are not allowed to wear headbands, leg sleeves, or arm sleeves. I'm not saying it's the only way or the right way, but it's a line we choose to hold.

Holding any standard is difficult, but this one is especially demanding because it is always challenged. The individuals on our teams, like every other human on Earth, think about themselves. But in order to be truly united as one, we must strike the perfect balance of considering the team as the priority while caring for ourselves enough to bring our best selves to the group. We will always get what we accept, so we can't flinch when holding our standard.

> CORE VALUE | Thankful
> MANTRA | "Touches."

In the context of our basketball program, the way we show love as an expression of our gratitude is by giving "touches"—any kind of physical contact between teammates, like high fives, a pat on the back, or helping a player up off the floor. In practice, we keep track of the number of touches between players, charting it as a statistic. A study conducted over a decade ago by researchers at the University of California, San Francisco, found a correlation between the number of physical touches between teammates and the success of a team.

We have a rule in our program: if a guy turns the ball over, everybody has to get a touch on him to help him move on from the error and focus on the next play. It's a simple gesture that connects our guys and shows appreciation for that teammate. Showing love, whether through touches or by writing thank-you notes, is an important way to exhibit gratitude. We do our best to intentionally honor the act.

Ryan's Mantras

> CORE VALUE | Thoughtful
> MANTRA | "Be still."

I learned years ago that I'm more thoughtful when I have stillness in my day. I must block out time on my calendar to reflect, to think, to wonder. I need that space to consider conversations I've had and ponder. Stillness is a critical part of being thoughtful.

CORE VALUE | Thankful
MANTRA | "Care deeply."

It seems obvious, but it's not. To leave people, places, and things better than you found them, you have to care. Nobody will know if you don't pick up the trash in the park. You have to care about the place to pick it up and make it better. Most people will never know about the calls made or the introductions facilitated on behalf of a person. You have to care deeply about helping people to consistently do those things.

CORE VALUE | Curious
MANTRA | "Fight complacency."

After things have gone well for a while, it's easy to sit back and rest on your laurels. It's almost natural to chill out and say, "I'm good. Let's put this in cruise control." That mindset goes against my values. I use the mantra "fight complacency" to remind myself never to go to that place. As a result of this focus on avoiding complacency, I struggle at times to celebrate accomplishments in life. It's hard to allow myself to slow down and relish the good things that have happened in my career because of my internal vigilance against complacency. Maybe, as I get older, I will get better at managing the friction between these two values. But for now, I'd rather err on the side of guarding against the lure of complacency.

CORE VALUE | Consistent
MANTRA | "Our level."

The phrase "our level" refers to the standard of excellence we have chosen to set for life. Not only do we show up every day no matter what, but we also do so with excellence. We don't just wander into the gym to lift weights and sit down between sets and take our time. We attack the weights with a vengeance. We employ a mindset that we are getting better that day and every day thereafter, just as we did every day before.

This mantra reminds me to ask myself, "Did I perform at a level of excellence today, or did I loaf?"

When I was playing football at Ohio University, every rep of practice was graded. For each play, you got one of four grades:

- + + Plus Plus (you made an extraordinary play, such as throwing a touchdown pass while scrambling away from an unblocked defensive lineman)
- + Plus (you did everything exactly as you were supposed to)
- – Minus (you didn't do your job exactly as you were supposed to)
- – – Double Minus (you made a mistake that hurt the team, like throwing an interception)

There was no neutral grade for doing things *almost* right. You didn't avoid a Minus grade by performing "close enough." The same is true off the field. This is about setting a standard and working hard *consistently* to live up to that standard each day. Living up to a standard is what creates the results we want. Setting a big goal doesn't do that. Results come from what we do each day. Performing at "our level" consistently is what creates the result.

BEAT MICHIGAN

Growing up in Ohio, it becomes ingrained in you to hate the University of Michigan. It started as a rivalry between football teams in 1897. Now you find people in Ohio crossing out the letter M in every word on signs or on their social-media profiles during the week of "The Game," as the

Ohio State/Michigan football game to end the regular season has come to be called. Some do it year-round. Fans from both schools revel in beating one another. There is even a clock in the Ohio State locker room that is always counting down until the next Michigan game.

In 1968, the game featured a titanic matchup: the number two–ranked undefeated Buckeyes hosting the number four–ranked one-loss Wolverines. At stake was the title of undisputed champion of the Big Ten conference and a date in the Rose Bowl against the top-ranked Trojans of Southern California. Under the leadership of Ohio State's legendary coach Woody Hayes, the Buckeyes blasted Michigan in the most lopsided post–World War II victory in the history of the rivalry (before or since). After a late touchdown run made the score 50–14 with under two minutes to play, Hayes called for a two-point conversion try instead of the normal extra-point kick. The pass fell incomplete, and after the game, reporters asked Coach Hayes why he went for two when the game was clearly in hand. "Because I couldn't go for three." Ohio State fans loved it. Even though some have disputed whether Hayes actually said this or not, the story lives on in Ohio State lore.

The following year, the Wolverines returned the favor. Led by new head coach and Woody Hayes protégé Bo Schembechler, Michigan upset Ohio State, ending the Buckeyes' twenty-two-game winning streak. In preparation for that game, Schembechler had everyone on the scout practice team wear the number 50 for the week to remind them of the previous year's humiliating defeat.[6] The Michigan win took the rivalry to another level, kicking off a period known as the "Ten-Year War."[7]

As mantras go, few are as recognizable as "Beat Michigan."

That said, and despite us being Ohio guys, we find that particular mantra—and rivalries between teams and people in general—to be shallow and uninspiring. Yes, we are aware of the research done by Simon Sinek and Adam Grant on some of the potential benefits of having a worthy rival (e.g., someone to measure yourself against and push you). But such a focus represents a fixation on an external scoreboard of comparison. It ties our value and self-worth to a single outcome. By elevating the importance of that single event, it devalues the process and all other events. This is contrary to what we believe.

Without a doubt, having a rival can act as a focusing lens, concentrating our energy and providing motivation in the short term. However, its benefit is fleeting and at odds with the goal of anyone seeking excellence, which isn't to simply beat a team or sell more books than someone else. It's to continually improve and be the absolute best version of ourselves each day. A focus on a single opponent is nothing more than comparison. Spending so much time and effort looking outward leaves little time to look inward, which is how we grow. Continuous improvement is what we're focused on. The funny thing about that posture is that it seems to impact the outer scoreboard in our favor as well.

RH: During my senior season at Centerville High School, our football team was having one of its greatest seasons ever. We were 8–0 and the top-scoring team in Ohio. We were set to play another 8–0 team, Wayne High School. It was billed the game of the year in the state. The *Dayton Daily News* ran a front-page story all five days of the week leading up to the game. For the game-day story in Friday's edition, they interviewed the quarterbacks of each team. On the front page of my hometown newspaper, there was a big picture of me and Derek Jones, the quarterback for Wayne. "It doesn't matter who shows up against us," I was quoted as saying. "It's about what we do. If we execute like we have all season, we'll be fine. The opponent doesn't matter." And that's what happened: we executed well and won the game 35–14.

A few weeks after the season was over, I was invited by a group of Wayne players to participate in a friendly backyard football game. I drove up to Huber Heights, and we played like little kids for hours in a park. It was so much fun. After we were done, everyone hung out and talked for a while. A few of their players commented on what I'd said about the game in the newspaper. "We read the paper that day and couldn't believe you didn't respect us enough to say our name," they said. "So many people at Centerville say 'Beat Wayne' that they had T-shirts made. We *loved* that. It meant we were in your head and you were thinking about us. It gave us confidence that you thought about us so much." Then they added, "When we saw that you said it didn't matter who showed up, it was intimidating. It had an effect on us."

What those would-be rivals said that day has stuck with me ever since. It is another example of why it's a waste of time to focus on an opponent or another person at work. It gives them confidence. Why do that? The benefits of focusing on yourself and what you do generate multiple positive effects. While rivalries are great for observers (who aren't in the game) and critics (who also aren't in the game), it's better for us—the people actually in the arena doing the work—to focus on what we do. We need to play to our own standards rather than worry about what a so-called rival is doing. Why waste mental energy on them when you could be focused on making yourself better?

TAKE ACTION

Exercise: Your Ethos

Why: To visualize your values

How: Select three images that represent who you are or who you want to be. Share and explain how the images relate to your core values and purpose to your team. Print out the pictures and display them where you'll see them daily.

Exercise: Your Mantra

Why: To affirm your values

How: Consider each of your core values and corresponding critical behaviors. Are there any sayings, quotes, people, or symbols that remind you of these values or behaviors? Think of these as the optimal version of your values. Select a single mantra for each core value.

CHAPTER 9

Excellence Is Mundane

The fight is won or lost far away from witnesses—behind the lines, in the gym, and out there on the road, long before I dance under those lights.

—Muhammad Ali

After delivering keynote speeches, we typically add extra time to answer questions from the audience. One of the most common is: "What are some quick hacks we can implement to be better leaders and/or win more games?" This question is understandable, given our instant-gratification, on-demand, "there's an app for that" culture. We live in a technological world where it is easy to hack our way to ordering food to eat, a ride to share, a house to rent, or a potential mate to date. Clickbait headlines and social-media influencers bombard us with messages that promise to reveal "the one trick" that will lead to more money in the bank, more results in the gym, and more happiness in life. Given all this, it isn't surprising that people want the quick answer to winning more games, getting a raise at work, and bettering their lives.

We understand the question. It's just that our answer is neither quick nor easy, and it isn't exciting to most. One of the differences between those who sustain excellence and those who don't is the ability to delay gratification. It is the willingness to suffer the monotony of showing up day after day to work on the little things that they trust will one day add up to something big. Delayed gratification supports the unremarkable and unoriginal work of endlessly mastering the fundamentals of one's craft.

This is an answer that often leaves the questioner visibly disappointed.

In the spring of 1989, sociology professor Daniel Chambliss published a paper titled "The Mundanity of Excellence." In it, he wrote:

> Superlative performance is really a confluence of dozens of small skills carefully drilled into habit and then are fitted together in a synthesized whole . . . Each of those tasks seems small in itself, but each allows the athlete to swim a bit faster . . . there is no secret; there is only the doing of all those little things, each one done correctly, time and again, until excellence in every detail becomes a firmly ingrained habit, an ordinary part of one's everyday life . . . Excellence is accomplished through the doing of actions, ordinary in themselves, performed consistently and carefully, habitualized, compounded together, added up over time.[1]

Chambliss's work calls to mind the philosophy of one of the most innovative and impactful coaches in all of professional sports: the San Francisco 49ers' legendary head coach, Bill Walsh. In his book *The Score Takes Care of Itself*, Coach Walsh wrote, "I directed our focus less to the prize of victory than to the process of improving—obsessing, perhaps, about the quality of our execution and the content of our thinking; that is, our actions and attitude. I knew if I did that, winning would take care of itself, and when it didn't, I would seek ways to raise our Standard of Performance."[2] The title of the chapter containing those words is among the most counterintuitive statements ever associated with an NFL head coach: "The Prime Directive Was Not Victory."

The unexciting truth is this: there are no hacks. Instead, there are daily actions adding up over time that lead to improvement. Stacking day after day after day gives you the chance to achieve any outcome-focused goal that you set for yourself. Setting victory, however you define it, as a goal doesn't help you achieve it. The system you implement to improve each day does. Want to earn a promotion? Behave as if you're interviewing for your next job each day (because you are). Want to win a state title? Practice with the focused intention of improving every single day. Want to write a book? Build yourself a system to get the words out of your head.

We read a story about how a group of authors formed a mastermind group to help them get their manuscripts done on time. One of the first guidelines they set for each other was this: every morning, for two hours, you are not allowed to do anything but write. You don't have to write, but you can't do anything else. One of the writers in the group said, "After a few minutes of just sitting there, I got bored and found that the words started coming out. That simple rule helped us get the work done."

If you want to set a big, audacious goal, that's fine. But what matters more is the system you create to help achieve it. What are the daily actions that, if done consistently, will lead to meeting the goal? That should be your focus. The mundane aspect of excellence is a beautiful thing for those willing to embrace it. As the desire for instant gratification continues to climb in the world, adopting this mindset is only becoming more of an advantage.

ENDURANCE > BRILLIANCE

As a fifteen-year-old, Eric Adams found himself in the basement of a four-story building in the section of Queens known as Jamaica. The building served as the headquarters for the 103rd Precinct of the New York City Police Department, home to some of the city's "most heavily patrolled streets."[3] Adams had been arrested for criminal trespassing: "unlawfully entering and remaining in the home of an acquaintance" is how he would describe it in a *New York Times* op-ed years later.[4] Before transferring Adams to spend the night in a juvenile detention center, the officers who arrested him repeatedly kicked him in the groin.

Adams wrestled with what to do with the experience. "For seven days after that, I stared into the toilet bowl in my house at the blood I was urinating. I kept telling myself that if it didn't clear up by the next day, I would share this shame and embarrassment with my mother." His traumatic story remained a secret he kept until he was an adult— working as a New York City police officer. He retired as a captain after twenty years and now serves as New York City's 110th mayor after a landslide electoral victory in 2021.

"You're going to go through some dark moments in your life," Adams's mother told him. "You have to make a determination if they are burials or plantings. You have to learn how to turn pain into purpose," she said about Adams's experience of being arrested, not knowing about the beating he had suffered. "I determined that that moment was not going to be a burial. It was going to be a planting,"[5] Mayor Adams said during his appearance on *The Learning Leader Show*.

It was only in college that Adams finally learned the source of his learning difficulties for which he had long been bullied as a kid. He had dyslexia, a language-processing brain disorder that makes it difficult to read. Once he learned about his dyslexia, Adams got the help he needed and continued to embrace hard work: "I knew that I would never beat you with brilliance. I am going to beat you with endurance. I'm not going to surrender. I'm going to continue to fight."

One of the keys to transforming yourself and others is generating the willingness to keep at it day after day. This means learning to enjoy the process of showing up each day, especially on the days when we don't feel like it, and enduring over time. It's the mindset employed by one of the greatest tennis players in history, Rafael Nadal (winner of twenty-two Grand Slam titles). In his autobiography, *Rafa*, he writes,

> One lesson I've learned is that if the job I did was easy, I wouldn't derive so much satisfaction from it. The thrill of winning is in direct proportion to the effort I put in before. I also know, from long experience, that if you make an effort in training when you don't especially feel like making it, the payoff is that you will win games when you are not feeling your best. That is how you win championships; that is what separates the great player from the merely good player.

Endurance matters. It is a life-trajectory force multiplier, whether life has handed you the trauma of an Eric Adams or the talent of a Rafael Nadal.

THE B+ STUDENT

Every high-school class in America has students who don't put forth their best effort. Another fact of high-school life is that within this low-effort segment of students, you will find one who barely engages, hardly turns in homework, and still ends up with an A. These students are smart, and because they know it, they know they can "succeed" at school without much effort.

In that same classroom, you can also find a student who is completely engaged. They take notes, ask questions, and study hard. They do all the work, give A-level effort, and end up earning a B+.

Now, consider this: Who would you rather have work for you?

If you compare them based solely on results—in the way that our society readily judges the efforts of any two people—the A student would be the choice. Hall of Fame football coach Bill Parcells is often quoted as saying, "You are who your record says you are." Based on that philosophy, the A student is better. But who do you want on your team? The A student who puts in minimal effort, misses assignments, and pays little attention to the details, or the B+ student who maximizes their potential by asking questions, working to understand, and turning over every stone to be their best? Seems like a pretty obvious answer in life.

You see, what's important to us is the process. We trust that if we are faithful to our process, the results will eventually follow. If they don't, either our process needs to be improved or our results don't reflect what's truly important. We prefer to focus on long-term thinking and sustainable results over time.

Besides, results now don't always mean results later. The B+ student will usually catch up to the A student over time through the persistence she is developing as part of the process.

We believe we are who our *process* says we are.

The *what* of our results is an expression of the *why* and *how* of our process. This isn't to say results don't matter. Obviously, they do. They simply matter less than the process used to get them. Living your core values is the cornerstone of your process. It's the pathway to living a life of excellence in which your definition of success rather than society's is fulfilled.

HANDLE HARD BETTER

The 1992 film *A League of Their Own* is a fictionalized account of the birth of the All-American Girls Professional Baseball League in 1943. Geena Davis plays Dottie Hinson, a catcher for the Rockford Peaches and the best player in the league. When we meet Dottie, she is perfectly content to stay where she is: working and playing softball for a local dairy in Oregon while she waits for her husband to return from the war. She has no interest in traveling to Illinois to play baseball professionally in this new league. She agrees to accept the league scout's invitation, however, on the condition that her younger sister, Kit, gets to do so as well. Kit, who is not as talented as Dottie, is desperate to leave rural Oregon and pursue a dream like this.

Over the course of the league's inaugural season, Dottie becomes the face of the league when a photo of her catching a foul ball while doing a split is featured on the cover of *LIFE* magazine. Sibling rivalry boils over as Kit erupts in jealous frustration at always being overshadowed by the taller, prettier, and more talented Dottie. The Peaches keep Dottie and trade Kit to the Racine Belles. By the end of the regular season, Dottie has led the Peaches to the league's best record and a spot in the World Series, where they will face Kit's Racine Belles.

As the movie drives toward its climax, one of the players leaves the team upon receiving the dreaded telegram informing her that her husband has been killed in action. That night, Dottie's husband surprises her after being wounded and discharged from the Army, upon which Dottie decides to quit and leave the team as well. As the team heads out to the bus to go to the World Series in the morning, the team manager, Jimmy Dugan, played by Tom Hanks, learns of Dottie's decision and confronts her.

"This is chickenshit, Dottie!" Jimmy says. "Sneaking out like this? Quitting? You will regret it for the rest of your life. Baseball is what gets inside you. It's what lights you up. You can't deny that." At this point in the movie, we have gotten to know Dottie as much as Jimmy has, and we know he is right. Dottie is not just good at playing baseball; playing baseball is a good thing for Dottie, as it has given her an experience of true joy, passion, and fulfillment.

"It just got too hard," Dottie tells Jimmy. Taking a step forward, Jimmy responds, "It's supposed to be hard. If it wasn't hard, everyone would do it. The hard is what makes it great."

Playing and competing on a great team is usually difficult. Each member of the team is asked to compromise their personal wishes and intentions for the good of the team in an endeavor of uncertain outcome. But being hard is precisely what makes it worth it. We all know it to be true, but our desire for comfort fools us into a life of compromise.

The leaders who have had the biggest impact on you had the highest expectations of you. The teacher who made the biggest difference in your life didn't let you skate by. The coach or boss who pushed you forward the most saw you for what you could be, not what you were, and then helped you become that. They gave you a reputation to live up to that was beyond what you thought of yourself.

Yes, it is hard. Accomplishing anything of value always is. Most people look for the easy way with the fewest obstacles. We search for hours for a hack or investigate every turn for a potential shortcut. The truth is this: *hard is the shortcut.* Hard makes us better. It prepares us for the future by challenging our present. It builds confidence and grit while making us question our resolve and fortitude. Reaching the summit of the mountain you trained months for, securing the client you studied and spent months getting to know, redeeming your team against that opponent that seemed to have your number the last few years—the pride we feel is the byproduct of the struggle.

Kara Lawson is a former WNBA player and Olympic champion. After her playing career ended, she worked as a broadcaster and NBA analyst for ESPN. She then left television to become the Boston Celtics' first female coach in their seventy-three-year history, and in 2020 she was hired to be the head women's basketball coach at Duke University. During a summer practice session to prepare for the upcoming 2022–23 season, Lawson addressed her team about the need to "handle hard better." In response to hearing players say how they were looking forward to getting through the grueling summer workouts because "it would get easier" once the season and school started in the fall, Lawson called her players together and urged them to shift their mindset. Here is part of what she said to them:

> We all wait in life for things to get easier . . . "Ah, I just gotta get through this and then it'll be easy." It's what we do. We wait for stuff to get easier.
>   It will never get easier. What happens is you handle hard better. That's what happens. Most people think that it's going to get easier—life is gonna get easier, basketball's gonna get easier, school's gonna get easier—it never gets easier. What happens is you become someone that handles hard stuff better. So that's a mental shift that has to occur in each of your brains. It has to. Because if you go around waiting for stuff to get easier in life, it's never going to happen . . . It's not going to get easier. It's gonna get harder. So make yourself a person that handles hard well. Not someone that's waiting for the easy. Because if you have a meaningful pursuit in life, it will never be easy . . . Any meaningful pursuit in life . . . goes to the people that handle hard well. Those are the people that get the stuff they want. People that wait around for easy? You'll probably see them at the bus stop. They're waiting . . . for the easy bus to come

around. Easy bus never comes around. You gotta handle hard. Okay? So don't get discouraged through this time if it's hard. Don't get discouraged. It's supposed to be. And don't wait for it to be easy . . . Make yourself someone who handles hard well.[6]

RH: Lawson reminds me of a coach I was fortunate to play for. Coach Ron Ullery was the offensive coordinator (and offensive line coach) at Centerville High School for twenty-two years prior to becoming the school's head coach in 2000. Coach Ullery has had as big an impact on me as any person in my life. It was from him that I learned the importance of high standards, resilience, preparation, and mental toughness. I asked him about his philosophy on leadership and why he was (and still is) so demanding of the people in his charge:

I'm a firm believer that most people "live up to or down to your stated expectations." And I also believe most young people set their expectations for themselves way too low. As a result, they become satisfied and content with their efforts, without ever nearing their actual potential. Our practice methods and demands were all based on proving to our players that they are capable of much more than they ever dreamed possible. I've always felt that this develops a "refuse to lose" mentality. If you work in a manner that you believe is harder than anyone else that will oppose you, you will be less likely to give in when adversity sets in, which, in the game of football, always does at some point. We always tried to put our players in situations in which they probably didn't feel like they could [succeed], and then push and demand of them that they do succeed. We tried to not give them an option of failing. Hence, running a play over and over until eleven players were perfect, starting practice over from the beginning because the effort and energy was lower than expected, not allowing players out of a one-on-one tackling drill until they had perfect technique and hit like a hammer no matter who they were, are examples of this. If we took all excuses away from the players, by accepting none, we felt the decision became theirs. Raise your level of effort and results above what you're willing to give, or we will continue until you do. The 4:30 AM, four-hour workouts, the forty-four forty-yard sprints, a timed mile, which was run every morning before 2-a-days until you reached a prescribed time, a championship circuit, which was four ten-minute stations of continuous high-level effort, were all examples of "conditioning" but also served as mentally toughening exercises. Most young people's response when told of these happenings is "I could never do that." However, like yourself, and all of your teammates, when not given an option to fail, they would also be able and willing to rise to a level they never thought they could rise to.

In addition to leading our offense and calling the plays, he personally coached our offensive line. Typically, the offensive coordinator coaches the quarterbacks as most people believe that is the most important position on the team. Not Coach Ullery:

I believe the leader of a team must be the hardest worker, the most driven, the most motivated, and the most dependable person in the group. The offensive line may not always be perceived as the leaders of a football team, but anyone that fully knows the game realizes that they are probably the most important part. They need to develop and exhibit these qualities. As they go, so goes the team. They are the least athletic players on the team, they are playing the position that is the absolute toughest to succeed at, it's the most physically demanding position, and it's the most important position on the field. To succeed at this position, your physical and mental toughness needs to be at an elite level. Offensive linemen will face more adversity in a game than any other position. They will not win every battle. As a matter of fact, they will lose a lot of individual battles in a game. How they respond to this adversity may be the greatest indicator of the success of the team in each game. I wanted practices for the offensive linemen to be so hard and demanding that they developed the toughness to embrace any challenge in front of them, no matter how daunting it seemed.

"Hard" has had a negative connotation for a long time. But hard is *great*. With no struggle, there is no pride in the accomplishment. What's beautiful about doing hard things is, eventually, we stop seeing them as hard. It just becomes what is. We stop categorizing and realize it doesn't matter whether we describe something as easy or hard; it just takes what it takes.

―――――――――――――― TAKE ACTION ――――――――――――――

Exercise: Letter to Adversity

Why: To appreciate setbacks

How: Write a thank-you letter to adversity as if it were a person. What positives have come out of the adversity? What has it taught you? Why are you thankful for it?

Exercise: Defining Success

Why: To gain clarity of your purpose

How: Reflect on the following two scenarios, then answer the questions that follow:

- A time when you were deemed successful by others but did not personally feel successful
- A time when you were deemed a failure by others but did not personally feel like a failure

What led to this discrepancy in each scenario? What are three things you can do to maintain your definition of success despite it being counter to society's definition?

CHAPTER 10

Humble and Hungry

Missing a train is only painful if you run after it. Likewise, not matching the idea of success others expect from you is only painful if that's what you are seeking.

—Nassim Taleb

The 2022 FIFA World Cup will be remembered by soccer fans worldwide as one of the best ever played. The biggest reason, of course, is how the global tournament ended. It featured an epic showdown between one of the world's great football powers, Argentina, and the defending World Cup champion, France. The teams were led by their superstar strikers: Argentina's Lionel Messi, arguably the greatest player of all time, versus France's Kylian Mbappé, arguably the greatest player of the present. The final had everything any fan of sport and excellence could ask for: a late rally by the champs to overcome a 2–0 deficit and send the game into extra time; the biggest stars rising to the occasion (Messi and Mbappé combined for three of the four goals in regulation, and then each scored again in extra time); jaw-dropping saves by the goalkeepers; and Messi finally winning his first World Cup in a penalty-kick shootout.

But in a tournament of endearing images, one of the most impactful took place in the locker room, not out on the field. On the fourth day of the tournament, long-time power Germany, with its four World Cup titles and sixty-eight wins in nineteen tournament appearances, opened its group-stage play against Japan. After giving up the first goal to Germany on a penalty kick in the first half, Japan entered the game's final fifteen minutes down 1–0. Eight minutes later, the unthinkable happened: Japan scored the second of two goals in quick succession. They held on to secure a shocking upset.

It was a monumental win for the Japanese team, and no one would have faulted them had they started their night of partying right away in the locker room. But that's not what happened. Following the game, the players shook hands with their opponent, celebrated together as a team, and then proceeded to *clean the locker room*. And by "clean," I don't just mean they picked up their stuff so the next team could use it. They left it better than they had found it. After the team departed Khalifa International Stadium in Doha, Qatar, World Cup reporters went into the locker room. It was *spotless*. The floors had been swept and all the towels folded. Not only that: the team left eleven origami cranes on the table along with a thank-you note in Japanese and Arabic for their hosts.[1]

Lest anyone think this was something unique with players on a team, one only needed to look out into the stands after Japan's epic win. With the excitement of having seen their country's most notable soccer victory in history still coursing through them, a group of Japanese fans grabbed trash bags and began picking up discarded bottles and food wrappers that littered the seating area as a way to show respect for their hosts.

This is nothing new or out of the ordinary for the Japanese. After seeing the kind gesture, media members searched their archives and found pictures of past Japanese locker rooms in 2018. What did they look like? Spotless, with a thank-you note to their hosts.[2] This was after a brutal 3–2 loss knocking them out of the World Cup. The loss was especially heart-wrenching because Japan had held a 2–0 lead with just over twenty minutes left to play. But when it was over, the Japanese didn't sulk, complain, or leave a locker-room mess in the wake of a devastating loss. They set that aside to show respect for their hosts by leaving their locker room cleaner than they'd found it.

It's not just about what you do. It's about how you do it. Japanese players and fans believe in showing respect and leaving places better than they found them. They don't talk about this; they just do it. That's leadership. That's living out values.

BC: For the last ten years, our basketball team has carried a broom with us to every away game we have played. We started doing this after being inspired by James Kerr's book *Legacy*, about the New Zealand All Blacks rugby team. The All Blacks are one of the winningest teams of all time in any sport, and one of their virtues is "sweeping the sheds." Our team's dustpan has this neatly written on it as a reminder. Following each game, our coaches or players sweep the locker room and be sure to leave it better than we found it. It takes a little extra time and effort, but it is a perfect application of our core values and a worthwhile way to live our values.

During our offseason in the fall, I like to watch football coaches conduct their practices. I love seeing how they organize their work, inspire their team's performance, and hold their players accountable. Over hundreds of practices, I've come to realize they are all saying basically the same things. The messages on tackling or blocking, for example, have different nuances, but the general meaning is pretty standard. The difference—and what separates the teams—is in how they deliver this messaging. About this, I don't just mean the coach's verbal execution or the pace at which they hold their practice. More than anything, I mean as it relates to who the coach is and what they value in their program. The performance of the coaches who align what they value on the field with what they say they value in the locker room far exceeds that of the others.

For example, if I say I value being tough, that needs to translate to something in practice. In our program, we know "tough" looks like positive body language. As such, our players must be held just as accountable for their body language as they are for boxing out for a rebound or screening to help get a teammate open. If I say we value being thankful, then I need to be aware of our guys giving each other high fives. I need to be sure we leave the weight room and opposing locker rooms nicer than we found them. I need to pick up trash and remind our players to do the same. Excellence will never be attainable unless and until our *how* for doing things is oriented with our *why* for doing them. One of the biggest mistakes a leader can make is thinking that these are secondary things. These are the main things.

WHERE DOES MOTIVATION COME FROM?

We believe that excellence is derived from internal rather than external motivation. However, all internal motivation is the byproduct of the story we tell ourselves. Unfortunately, we often lack the awareness that the story we tell ourselves needs to be intentional, lest our motivation be inconsistent and unfocused.

If you think of motivation as fuel for action, the purest fuel comes from narratives of fulfillment. These stories revolve around our internal desires to become the best version of ourselves because that's what we are supposed to do. For some, this obligation arises out of a duty to God; for others, it is simply seen as the only logical way to live a life worth living. In any case, the story is pure, consistent in direction, and focused solely on the person telling it.

There is an optimism to these narratives. They are tales of hope focused on the positive: what we can accomplish, achieve, and do. Affirmations pertaining to jobs and positions we want to attain, goals we are working to meet, or dreams we want to realize are all examples of positive fuel. They provide hope through stories that reinforce that we can have what we want as long as we keep working to make it happen.

Negative fuel built from narratives of refute can also be effective. In these stories, we are driven by an unquenchable thirst to prove someone wrong. Perhaps it arises from a parent's criticism, a coach's harsh judgment, or being dismissed by a boss who said we weren't good enough. Negative fuel can come from a teacher who said we weren't "college material" or the girlfriend who laughed when we said we wanted to write a book. Whatever the source, these types of stories are all about overcoming the doubt of someone else. Seven-time Super Bowl champion Tom Brady was motivated by his doubters:

> I always deal with people that doubt me better . . . I love when they give me a little more fuel for the fire . . . and I think there's a good emotion in sport . . . There's an *anger* when you play that is a really motivating factor, too, because it sparks an *action*. Anger motivates you to, you know, wake up sometimes and dig deep. And I love digging deep because I learn a lot about myself, and I think when we dig deep and people push us further than places we want to go, you know, we can reach places that [people] have never been.[3]

It should be noted that these stories don't necessarily have to be true in order to be valuable as motivation; we just have to believe them. Michael Jordan, considered by many to be the greatest basketball player of all time, was notorious for creating stories for himself about opposing players who made him feel slighted or disrespected in some way. The "Nobody respects me!" chip on one's shoulder is a common tool for motivation in competition, regardless of the sport.

But this applies to positive fuel as well. A complimentary word of encouragement from somebody we respect can infuse us with the confidence to do the things that confirm the validity of those words of praise, even if they weren't objectively true when they were said.

Both positive and negative fuel involve elements of comparison and thus should be used with caution. Comparison-based motivation is like a campfire. If diligently maintained and supervised, it can provide much-needed light and warmth and can serve as a cooking resource. However, if a campfire is not watched closely, its flame can burn out of control. Before you realize what has happened, a forest fire has erupted that requires major work to get under control. Make use of comparison-based motivation with great care.

The beauty of motivation is that it enables us to overcome obstacles. If our motivation, or purpose, is strong enough, adversity becomes manageable. No longer do we view the process as long or difficult; it just becomes what it takes. Motivation can cure almost all ills.

GOING FOR IT

When the opportunity to perform presents itself, it comes with a choice. How much should you push the boundaries of what is comfortable versus tread carefully in light of possible failure? Brook found himself facing that choice the first time Ryan asked him to speak at one of Ryan's Learning Leader Growth Summits.

BC: I remember sitting there thinking to myself, *What does a high-school basketball coach have to say to a group of business leaders and CEOs?* I got into this mindset of *What the hell? Why not just go for it?*

Who cares if they think I'm an idiot? What does it matter? I detached from looking for approval pretty quickly. I remember thinking, *Let's go. I'm just gonna go.* I had people doing crazy handshakes and all types of improv exercises. It could have been received terribly.

To me, this is where all the juice in life is. When I tune in to *American Idol* or some reality show and get goosebumps from watching someone's performance, those goosebumps are a result of witnessing someone really go for it. Or when you watch kids play games and they're putting everything they have into it, playing so hard that they have nothing left—now that's what it's all about. Not scholarships or trophies, just surrendering the outcome and going for it. If your foundation doesn't give you access to the courage to be real, you won't have much juice, and without juice, the people around you won't feel safe to be themselves and give their best.

RH: Whenever I have played it safe because I was scared or nervous about looking stupid, the result has never been anything remarkable, memorable, or impactful. Those performances may not have been objectively bad, failures, or losses. They were adequate, worthy of a passing grade, but that's about it.

However, when I've embraced the risk of looking dumb and really gone for it—whether by doing a big keynote opening to get the group excited, telling the joke to get the audience laughing, or sharing the maybe-too-personal story to get the leader's attention—those are the times people remember. I know because I've had them come up to me afterward and say, "Man, you really went for it." To me, that's the juice. That's the good stuff.

Going for it means running the risk of embarrassing yourself in order to do something extraordinary. The higher the payoff at the end, the larger the risks you must take to get it. Sometimes going big leads to absolutely flopping, but playing it safe means never having the chance to pull off something worth talking about.

BC: One of the best athletes I've ever had the privilege of watching epitomizes "going for it." It will probably surprise you to learn that this person is a wrestler and our babysitter . . . oh, yeah, and now an Olympic gold medalist. He also happened to be a part of one of the best sporting events I've ever witnessed—a high-school wrestling match at St. Paris Graham High School in 2009. I was the athletic director and boys' basketball coach at Graham at the time, and we were hosting Lakewood St. Edward's High School, a matchup that would have national-championship implications. As if that wasn't enough to garner significant interest, Graham's three-time defending state champion, David Taylor, chose to move up a weight class in order to face St. Ed's three-time defending state champion, Collin Palmer. I was matside as the sold-out crowd was treated to two incredible high-school athletes laying everything on the line simply to test themselves. Obviously, Taylor moving up a weight class in order to set up the match was the ultimate throwing down of the gauntlet. The match of the century, as it was dubbed by high-school sports writers, was tight throughout. Despite jumping out to quick 2–0 lead on a takedown in the first thirty seconds of the match, Palmer fell to Taylor 8–5, with Taylor securing the win with two back points late in the third period. Both young men went on to win their fourth Ohio state wrestling championship later that year.

Taylor's appetite for "going for it" was just getting started. He followed his stellar high-school career with an elite collegiate career in which he advanced to the national championship match in his weight class all four years. His freshman year ended with a disappointing finals loss, following an unbeaten season to that point. In Taylor's sophomore year, he moved up a weight class, claimed his first national title, and was named the Dan Hodge Trophy winner as the best collegiate wrestler in the country. His junior season ended in a heartbreaking championship, a 5–4 loss to Cornell legend and senior Kyle Dake, who capped his career off with his fourth NCAA title. Taylor bounced back again in his senior campaign running off an undefeated season to capture his second national championship and become only the third multiple winner of the Dan Hodge Trophy.

Of course, as someone who has structured his entire life around chasing excellence, Taylor was not finished. He had more to give to the sport and further limits to push himself to. So, he set his sights on the Olympics. Taylor's resilience would be put to the test, but by this point his motivation and willingness to run to, and through, challenges were cemented in his character. Just take a look at his path to an Olympic gold medal.

- 2012: US Trials finishes 3–2 (summer Olympic year)
- 2013: US Trials loss to Kyle Dake in finals
- 2014: US Trials loss to Dake in finals
- 2015: US Trials loss to Dake in finals
- 2016: US Trials loss to Dake in finals (*summer Olympic year*)
- 2017: US Trials loss to J'den Cox in finals
- 2018: US World Champion and member of US World/Olympic Team
- 2019: Knee injury; forfeits US World Team position
- 2020: US World Champion and member of US World/Olympic Team (summer Olympic year)
  - Olympics canceled due to COVID-19

The 2020 Olympic Games were rescheduled for 2021. Taylor was finally going to have the opportunity to compete for his country on the biggest stage in the world. And he was certainly going to go for it. Taylor was in full command throughout the first three rounds, beating all three opponents by technical fall—think "mercy rule" for those unfamiliar with wrestling. His finals pairing, however, was a different story, as he matched up with Hassan Yasdani of Iran. Yasdani was the reigning world and Olympic champion. I clearly remember standing in my living room in the early morning—leaning, twisting, and yelling at the television as the match came down to the wire. Trailing 2–3 late in the third period and clearly exhausted, both Taylor and Yasdani were struggling to mount much offense given the clear advantage to Yasdani, who was in the lead. But, unwilling to submit, Taylor again chose to go for it. With just under twenty seconds remaining in his first-ever Olympic gold-medal match, Taylor hit a two-point takedown that sent him to the top of the podium and secured his place among wrestling folklore forever.

Not bad for a babysitter moonlighting as a wrestler.

Coming up short so many times was undoubtedly disappointing, but it comes with the "going for it" mentality. If you can't handle failure and disappointment, get out now. It did not matter that he had been ultra successful by virtually everyone else's standards. It was Taylor's opinion of himself that mattered. He was the one who knew what he was capable of—only him. His resolve, and obligation, to become the best version of himself was more powerful than any disappointment. Only his inner scoreboard could provide this unique perspective.

PUSH YOUR PACE

Excellence is all about striving for your personal best. Success, on the other hand, is about coming out on top in a comparison with others, regardless of whether it involves your best or theirs. In order to elevate our aim from mere success to a higher standard of excellence, we need to address the difference between what is accepted and what is possible.

It's acceptable to play full-court defense and pressure the ball sometimes. It's acceptable to push the pace on offense sometimes. It's acceptable to run in transition the majority of the time. It's exactly what most teams do.

It's acceptable to have a positive attitude at work most of the time. It's acceptable to be mentally and physically present with your family most of the time. It's acceptable to meet the deadline for your project or to get to work right on time. They're all acceptable approaches to succeeding at the task at hand. But excellent they are not.

Consider the alternative of acceptable: what is *possible*. It's possible to pick up full court and pressure the ball every time. It's possible to push the pace on offense in transition every time. It's possible to sprint the floor every time. Few teams do it because it's hard. But it's possible. It's possible to have a positive attitude at work every day, regardless of what happened that morning or the previous day. It's possible to be engaged with your family every time you are together. It's possible to complete projects before the deadline and show up early to work. It's not easy, but it's possible. The idea that it's hard is exactly what scares most people away and draws those desiring excellence.

You can succeed by doing what is acceptable, but excellence is hard. Consistency is hard. But it's possible. Consistency is one of the most distinguishing characteristics of excellence. And it is consistency that society struggles with the most. We celebrate the singular moment of crowning achievement without paying homage to the years of strain and struggle that made it possible. Those willing to embrace the persistent, unheralded work of doing the *possible* are on the path to excellence in business and in life.

TAKE ACTION

Exercise: Teammate Reflection

Why: To grow humility

How: Think of the worst teammate you've ever had. Make a list of what this person did that made them such a poor teammate. Do the same for the best teammate you've ever had. Is there anything from the worst-teammate list that you currently do? What are the three things from the great-teammate list that you could start doing?

Exercise: Farmer's Alliance

Why: To appreciate the extra

How: Watch the 2013 "Farmer" Ram Trucks commercial.[4] Consider your job or role in life. What do you do above and beyond your job description that most people wouldn't know about? Create a similar narrative to the Ram Trucks commercial to describe your position.

CHAPTER 11

Gratitude Triumphs

Most beliefs are self-validating. Angry people look for problems and find them everywhere, happy people seek out smiles and find them everywhere, pessimists look for trouble and find it everywhere. Brains are good at filtering inputs to focus on what you want to believe.

—Morgan Housel[1]

University of Florida women's soccer coach Becky Burleigh knew that the weight of expectations could overwhelm a team's ability to perform at its best. The pressure of achieving something memorable could turn hope into anxiety. This was especially a concern for her team heading into the NCAA tournament in 2014. Of the twenty players who would eventually log any time on the field over the course of the Gators' run through the tournament, nearly half were seniors. For them, the prospect of an abrupt "one and done" exit from the postseason would be especially hard. Not only would it mark the dashing of their championship hopes, but it would also mean the end of their college playing careers.[2]

As Coach Burleigh would later say on *The Learning Leader Show*,[3] fear of failing can lead us to seek excuses ahead of time that will explain the failure. Then, with those excuses in place, players' performances tend to become tentative. To go deep into the tournament, her Gators would need to "go all in and play free." To get her players mentally ready to do that, regardless of the circumstances or the opponent they faced, Coach Burleigh introduced the mantra "Go green." Using the metaphor of a traffic light and its green = go system, she presented the team with green gift bags containing green armbands. The system was simple: when adversity struck or a mistake was made, the sight of the armbands and the exhortation of teammates to "go green" would remind the player to not dwell on it. Move on, stay aggressive, and keep taking the risks necessary to succeed.

After winning their first three tournament games, the Gators were set to face off against the number three–ranked team in the nation, Stanford, in the Elite Eight quarterfinals. This team had dominated throughout the season, having outscored its opponents on its home field 34–2. Stanford had every reason to be confident that if they scored first, winning would be a near certainty.

Which is exactly what happened: Stanford scored the game's first goal just 3:21 into the match.[4] To be losing so soon into the game could easily have led to fear taking over at that point. Instead, the Gators rallied around their mantra. On the sideline, players began taking their green wristbands off and waving them in the air. One shouted, "This is when we're louder than ever!" Just over six minutes later, the Gators celebrated their own goal. The game was tied 1–1.

It would remain that way until late in the game. With roughly fifteen minutes left to play, Stanford scored again. Once again, Stanford had what felt like an insurmountable one-goal lead. But once again, the

Gators fell back on their mantra: get back to green. This time, it took them just four minutes and fifteen seconds to answer with another game-tying goal. Neither team would score again, either in regulation or in the two extra time periods. Ultimately, the game was decided on penalty kicks. Stanford advanced to the Final Four. Florida's run was over.

But their mantra had taken root. It became part of Gator culture. The players took to using a green Sharpie marker to draw a green dot on their forearm when an armband wasn't available. The team even incorporated a button-sized green dot into the design of their jersey the following season.[5] The sight of a single color or the utterance of a simple two-word phrase—"Go green!"—helped reset their focus on the value the team had previously determined to be necessary for success: being unafraid to take risks.

LOVE LANGUAGES

"The need for significance is the emotional force behind much of our behavior," writes Gary Chapman. His book *The Five Love Languages* has become a cultural marvel since its publication in 1992. Through his love-language model, assessment, and tools, Chapman has helped millions better understand themselves and their closest loved ones when it comes to this most basic, fundamental need. "We want our lives to count for something. We have our own idea of what it means to be significant, and we work hard to reach our goals. Feeling love . . . enhances our sense of significance."[6]

While Chapman's words were about the communication of love between spouses, his framework has found application across a wide spectrum of interpersonal relationships. Leaders in a professional setting are asking "What's your love language?" of the people they lead. For example, take Jesse Cole, owner of one of the more unique professional baseball teams, the Savannah Bananas.

Since being purchased by Cole and his wife, Emily, the Bananas have been compared to the Harlem Globetrotters: a unique fusion of sports and entertainment performance playing to packed stadiums wherever they go. The Bananas have welcomed more than one million fans to Grayson Stadium, their home park in Georgia, which has a seating capacity of just four thousand and has hosted the likes of Babe Ruth, Lou Gehrig, Hank Aaron, Ty Cobb, and Jackie Robinson during their minor-league and exhibition-playing days. The team has been featured on HBO, CNN, *CBS Sunday Morning*, and the *Los Angeles Times* and has even had their own show on ESPN. The Bananas have currently sold out every game of their upcoming season and have a waiting list of more than 300,000.

There are many reasons behind the phenomenon Jesse and Emily built. Some might say it's their viral social-media videos. "Bananaball," as the team calls its performances, is tailor-made for a TikTok world. But for Jesse, it all starts with how he treats his people.

Cole had each team member take the Five Love Languages assessment and learned that most of his employees have "words of affirmation" as their top love language. As a result, he implemented new verbiage within the team. For example, his executive assistant received the new title of "Executive Rockstar." His motto? "Do for one what you wish you could do for many." That means finding seemingly simple but intentional ways to show someone that they and their contributions to the team are significant.

RH: Jesse frequently texts me a video message sharing what he loved about one of my recent podcast episodes and how it impacted his life in a positive way. I'm sure he does this for many people. As a leader, Cole has learned how the important people in his life feel love, and then he loves them like crazy. The entire operating principle behind how he runs the Bananas is a giant expression of love to the team's fans. Every innovative idea that is tried is because Cole and his team believe it will improve the experience for the fans attending their games. This includes everything, both on the field (i.e., if a fan catches a foul ball on the fly, it counts as an out) and off it (every ticket to Grayson Stadium includes all-you-can-eat concessions).

Another example: Cole didn't like how the ballpark looked with advertisements throughout the stadium. More importantly, he believed it cheapened the experience for his fans. So he removed the ads. All of them. By erasing every advertisement from the stadium grounds and experience, the team lost hundreds of thousands of dollars in advertising revenue. But in Cole's eyes, it's money well spent. "I wanted to give the stadium back to the fans," he said.

Messages like Cole's make me feel significant, so it was no surprise that words of affirmation scored a close second place when I took the Love Languages assessment. I scored highest on quality time, which I didn't understand at first.

Then one night earlier this year, I was having a conversation with my wife, Miranda, about how we give and receive love. We were talking about our days as well as what we were excited for in the future. As she asked me more questions about the current projects I was working on, upcoming podcast guests, and this book, I paused for a second and said, "My love language is curiosity. I feel seen, heard, and loved when you ask questions about what I'm working on and excited about. That's my actual love language." What I was expressing falls squarely within the concept of quality time as Chapman describes it. "If I am sharing my love for you by means of quality time," he writes, "and we are going to spend that time in conversation, it means I will focus on drawing you out, listening sympathetically to what you have to say. I will ask questions, not in a badgering manner but with a genuine desire to understand your thoughts, feelings, and desires."[7] Curiosity, it appears, is better described as the particular dialect of the love language of quality time that I resonate with the most.

I was reminded of this during my conversation with Julia Boorstin. Boorstin is the senior tech and media correspondent for CNBC. Her parents raised her to show respect for others by asking questions. Boorstin told me, "Asking questions is a sign of respect, and it shows that you care."[8] Showing a genuine interest and asking questions is the most effective way to build a deep relationship quickly with someone else. To do this, you must find people and their stories endlessly fascinating. For me, it helps that my daily work revolves around asking fascinating people thoughtful questions. It's a reminder that I'm doing the work that I was meant to do.

We all have the potential to find people fascinating and to be curious enough to learn more about them. It is a learned skill. It's not something I felt earlier in my life. I've developed it as I've matured and grown more interested in people and their stories. Not only is it a fulfilling way to live, but it also gives you the best opportunity to deepen your relationships with others.

A TEAM VOCABULARY

Metaphors are like crowbars. A few words enable understanding of a larger, more complex idea. The mantra of "Go green," as Burleigh explained, was inspired by a mundane traffic light.

Using a metaphor can give your team a common vocabulary that is rich with meaning. Consider how the different colors of a traffic light can be used to increase awareness of the personal energy a person is bringing to the team and how it impacts the group.

- Green: You are positive and confident about where the team is going and the role your effort plays in getting there. You are ready to go. Your foot is on the gas, adding acceleration to the team's momentum.

- Yellow: You are a bit shaky. Excuses start to creep in to justify a lack of full effort or for not completely showing up with intention and intensity. Your foot is no longer on the gas. You are coasting, adding nothing to the team's momentum.
- Red: You are actively contributing negative energy. Perhaps you are displaying a victim mentality, have started blaming others, or have totally checked out. Your foot is on the brake, working against the team's momentum.

Giving your team members a common vocabulary helps them stay the course and keep each other focused on it. It gives them a point of reference with which to support each other. "Hey, man, you're yellow. Let's get back to green." "I'm having a red-light day, and I need help."

As leaders, we have a heightened responsibility to be aware of and intentional about the color we are bringing every day because our teams are going to be colored by it. We are either adding energy to the space and to our people or taking it away. When you make the choice to lead, you no longer get to be energy neutral. When you choose to lead, the energy you project becomes part of your responsibility. When you walk into a meeting, the team is watching. Whether through conscious thought or subconscious feeling, they are attuned to the question "What type of energy are you bringing to this?" *There is no yellow for leaders.* You have to think about it consciously before entering any room: *I am either green and adding, or I'm red and taking away.*

Performance consultant Dr. Kevin Elko introduced a few effective phrases during his work with the University of Alabama football team that illustrate team vocabulary at its finest. Phrases such as "So What Now What" and "Be Where Your Feet Are" became part of the fabric of the Crimson Tide program and a tool that allowed them to release themselves from a mistake and move back into the present moment.

THANKFUL THURSDAYS

Regardless of our love language, having another human being express gratitude to us *for us* is a powerful gift. Gratitude has the capacity to generate important neurochemicals. When thinking shifts from negative to positive, there is a surge of feel-good chemicals such as dopamine, serotonin, and oxytocin. These all contribute to the feelings of closeness, connection, and happiness that come with gratitude.[9] But those brain benefits aren't just for the recipient of gratitude. Expressing gratitude works similarly for the person giving thanks.

Ask yourself: How often do you text, call, or write someone a note with the sole intention of saying you're grateful for them? When you express gratitude to someone, how specific are you?

A crucial aspect of being intentional about telling someone you're thankful for them is being specific about why.

BC: In our leadership classes, we have a few things that are daily routines. One element that never wavers is our Thankful Journal. We begin every class every day by writing down three things we are thankful for. The topics vary from weekend activities to former teammates to your favorite cartoon growing up, but the topic is secondary to the process of reflecting and considering what you are genuinely thankful for. Like the endorphins our bodies release when working out, acknowledging gratitude releases similar feel-good chemicals.[10]

Every Thursday, we have each student text three people they're thankful for—one older, one roughly the same age, and one younger—and share why they're thankful for them. These Thankful Thursdays have a specific purpose. If you know you're going to send three text messages every Thursday to recognize someone else, you will always be on the lookout for people you are grateful for. You become more observant, present, and intentional. This weekly cadence of self-imposed, scheduled expectation acts as a forcing function, pushing you to be a more active participant both as someone doing the work and noticing others who are doing it well. It's important to understand that feeling gratitude isn't the same as expressing it. Being thankful and not sharing it is like buying someone a present and leaving it in your closet. We want to seize the opportunity to lift others up.

In this light, we take Thankful Thursdays one step further by making cold calls. In a cold call, a student in class identifies someone they are grateful for and then calls them. When the person answers, the student expresses their gratitude and explains why that warranted taking the step of calling to tell them so. All of this is done on speakerphone in front of the whole class. Obviously, the responses vary significantly, but one thing is very clear: the person receiving the call is happy to have been chosen. They've been lifted up by a specific, intentional, surprise act of gratitude. It never misses.

"TIMES LEFT"

Cassie Holmes is a professor at UCLA's Anderson School of Management, where she studies the intersection of time and happiness. She teaches a popular MBA course called "Applying the Science of Happiness to Life Design." For the rest of us, she has packaged these learnings into her book, *Happier Hour: How to Beat Distraction, Expand Your Time, and Focus on What Matters Most.*

When she spoke with Ryan on *The Learning Leader Show*, Holmes talked about the implications of her research: "Life circumstances [like wealth, marital status, home ownership, and attractiveness] that we don't have a lot of control over have some effect [on happiness] but a surprisingly small one."[11] Instead, research shows that "what we do, how we spend our time, and how we approach that time" has a vastly greater impact on happiness. This is great news since that's what we have the most control over.

At the beginning of each course, Professor Holmes polls her students, asking them to identify their greatest source of pride and their greatest source of regret. Over the years, three-quarters of the time, the answer is the same: their greatest source of pride is relationships with the people they care most about. Conversely, their greatest source of regret comes from not spending more time with them. The takeaway is clear: we are acutely aware, both positively and negatively, of the impact investing our time in the people we care about has on the quality of our lives.

To help us focus on this, Holmes shared an exercise she described as the Counting Times Left exercise. Think of an activity that brings you joy and ask yourself how many more times in your life you can expect to do it given how often you do it (or fail to) now. This question is especially piercing when focused on what has the greatest impact on our happiness: our relationships. How many times have you had one-on-one time with your daughter in the past year? How many walks have you gone on with your spouse? How many meals have you shared with your mom and dad? How many times have you done it in the past month? How many more times do you have left? Realize that it's probably not that many. That realization will help you cherish the time and be intentional about maximizing its use on what matters most.

Author Tim Urban writes about going through the same mental exercise with regard to the time he realistically has left with his parents, who are both in their mid-sixties. It's worth reading in full:

> During my first 18 years, I spent some time with my parents during at least 90% of my days. But since heading off to college and then later moving out of Boston, I've probably seen them an average of only five times a year each, for an average of maybe two days each time. 10 days a year.
>
> . . . Being in their mid-60s, let's continue to be super optimistic and say I'm one of the incredibly lucky people to have

both parents alive into my 60s. That would give us about 30 more years of coexistence. If the ten days a year thing holds, that's 300 days left to hang with mom and dad. Less time than I spent with them in any one of my 18 childhood years.

When you look at that reality, you realize that despite not being at the end of your life, you may be nearing the end of your time with some of the most important people in your life. If I lay out the total days I'll ever spend with each of my parents—assuming I'm as lucky as can be—this becomes starkly clear: It turns out that when I graduated from high school, I had already used up 93% of my in-person parent time. I'm now enjoying the last 5% of that time. We're in the tail end.[12]

The marketing team behind Ruavieja, a Spanish spirits company, captured this in a powerful way. In a YouTube video,[13] they brought together a series of two people who have some form of relationship. Some are friends. Some are parents and children. Some live in the same city. Some live farther apart. The commonality among all is that the relationships they have are important to both parties. The interviewer asks them how often they see each other. Then they do a calculation based on the current amount of time they see one another that estimates how many more times they'll see each other in their lives. The result? Everyone is shocked. The number of times they will see that important person in their life is far less than they imagine. And they make a pact to spend more time together. Most of us don't realize how much time we waste on what's not important, and, in turn, we neglect our most important relationships. It's on us to be intentional about deepening those relationships. The best way to do that? Time.

BC: One of the greatest moments of my life was marked by two, ten-second hugs.

A life of basketball together had led us to the University of Dayton and the state championship game. Beyond what either of us could have dreamed, when the buzzer sounded, we had just won the first state championship in our school's history. The court was a frenzy of players running from teammate to teammate, embracing in joy. I had already celebrated with the coaches and a few players who were nearby. I looked up and saw my son, Gabe, running out of a pack of players toward me. We met around half-court in a hug that expressed more than words ever could. Neither of us said anything besides "I love you." For those ten seconds, I was just Dad. Shortly after that was followed by another ten-second hug with the other two people who had experienced all the ups and downs with us, my wife Betsy and daughter Ally.

Coaching your son is such a blessing. The opportunity to tie so many of your life experiences together is so unique and special, but one of the things you have to sacrifice is some of your time as Dad. Coach and Dad cannot be the same person. At this point, Gabe and I had been doing this dance for a long time. He had always handled it with a grace and toughness any father would be proud of. Of course, I had rarely told him this. I was too busy being a coach. During the hug, I couldn't think of anything other than how proud I was of Gabe. He honored his values of being selfless, devoted, and joyful. He cared about his teammates and the guys who had come before him. He played the game the right way. He was constantly showered with hate because he was the coach's son and had played with Bronny James growing up, yet he never buckled, never gave in to it. And he worked. Always once, usually twice, often three times a day. And here I was, his dad and his coach, standing on the court following a state championship game, hugging him. Then, together, we made our way over to the two people who were our support system. Two people who never wavered on their belief in us and love for us. I'll never forget it.

I find it fascinating that entitlement and arrogance are rooted in outcomes, while humility and confidence are married to the process. When immersed in the process of improvement, we can see our own shortcomings clearly. An affection for outcomes leads us to dismiss, rather than accept, those shortcomings.

Gratitude and love. Isn't it funny how we always return to these humble virtues? We would be best served if we never departed from them.

THE F-IT BUTTON

There may not be anything as important as how you respond to failure. If you choose to lead, it's inevitable that tough moments will come your way. It's going to happen, and to perform well over time, you have to find a way to deal with moments of failure, stress, or high emotion. What do you do to regroup when things go bad?

Staying present in the moment is a huge part of any competitive sport, especially during live competition—which describes much of our world at work. Fear is in the future. It's never in this moment; it's focused on what might happen. Anger is in the past: we get mad after we make a mistake or react to something that just happened. In fear or anger, we are taken out of the present moment. The more we can live in the present, the better we can be. Brook has printed shirts for members of our Learning Leader Circle with an "F" on the chest. Whenever there is a setback, you touch the "F-it button" ("Forget it," but you can use a different "F" word if that works for you). You touch that "F" as a way to quiet the voice of the inner critic who tends to speak after a failure. Sometimes a physical action can help reset that and push it from the present into the past.

BC: Our team borrowed this idea from Brett Ledbetter and, I believe, the Florida Gators track team. Whenever a failure occurs, whether large or small, we want our players to simply slap their chests, leave the failure behind, and focus on the next play. Then they should show each other love—especially after bad plays where mistakes were made—by giving each other high fives or touches. Together, these make up our failure-recovery system. It's now grown to an individual practice in which we help players create their own system.

Your failure-recovery system can be anything. It's a good exercise for anyone, but especially leaders, to think of a physical action you can do in moments when you need to respond with grace. Having a plan in place beforehand allows you to be proactive rather than reactive in those moments of adversity.

RESETTING FOR TOMORROW

As part of the process of continuous growth, it is useful to practice regular reflection and analysis of what is going well, what is not, and, most importantly, why. You know those times when you meet someone and it's immediately apparent that they are comfortable in their own skin? The ones who seem to truly know themselves? The ones not driven by insecurities? They have an ease about how they move in the world because they seem to have a complete understanding of themselves. Those people likely spend time reflecting on their core values and how their behaviors align with them, understanding why they've done well and why they've messed up.

We do this through journaling. There isn't a right or wrong way to go about this. For example, Ryan prefers to journal at night as a way to close each day. Brook, on the other hand, journals in the morning about how he did the previous day as a way to set his focus for the day ahead. Find the rhythm, setting, and angle that works best for you. But it can't be overstated: the process of writing down your thoughts is extremely important. We are believers in the adage "How can I know what I think until I see what I write?" Writing sharpens your reasoning and helps create clarity of thought. All leaders should have a writing practice. We share our routines below not as a prescription but as examples for your consideration.

RH: I'm a prompt-driven thinker and writer. Responding to something catalyzes my thinking much more than an empty page does. This is why I like the question-and-answer session after keynote speeches. The questions people ask force me to think quickly and share a useful answer immediately.

At the end of each day, I ask myself the following questions to reflect on whether or not I'm growing.

1. Am I a little bit wiser going to bed tonight than I was when I woke up this morning?

This comes from one of my favorite Charlie Munger quotes: "I constantly see people rise in life who are not the smartest, sometimes not even the most diligent, but they are learning machines. They go to bed every night a little wiser than they were when they got up and boy does that habit help, particularly when you have a long run ahead of you."[14] So, I ask myself: What did I do today to ensure that I'm a little bit wiser? What books did I read? What mentors did I meet with? What did I learn from this interview? What did I learn from the podcasts I listened to? What did I learn from the actions I took today?

2. What did I do today to push my edges?

This question is about living at the edges of my current comfort and competency zone. What did I do today that scared me? What did I do today that expanded my comfort zone? This is the only way we grow. When we live inside the comfortable little box of life, doing things that are easy, don't force us to push, and don't make us a little bit scared, we don't grow. Who did I talk to today that made me rethink a position I had on something? What physical action did I take that made my body push beyond its current capabilities? What room did I show up in where everyone else was smarter than I? Taking deliberate action to push your edges is when growth happens. We have to be intentional to ensure this occurs because we won't stumble into it by accident. We are conditioned to take the easier route, not the harder one.

These end-of-day prompts ensure that I don't lie to myself. When I keep stacking days of answering those questions with the affirmative, I seem to create more opportunities to work with amazing people, help others more, and get luckier. It's weird how that works.

BC: Journaling as part of my self-reflection process is something I've grown to treasure. It took me a few years to find a system that fit me best, but now I have a process that allows me to reflect on, evaluate, and reconnect with my true self quickly and concisely. Here is my daily process:

- **Reflect on and evaluate** core values. For each value question, I give myself a star (above the standard), a check mark (at the standard), or a dash (below the standard). Then I make note of anything particularly good or bad regarding my core values from the previous day.
  - Tough: Did I maintain positive body language?
  - Passionate: Did I choose to do extra work?
  - Unified: Did I speak and act with urgency?
  - Thankful: Did I show love?
- **Reconnect** with personal mantra and affirmations.
  - "I laugh at fear, afraid of nothing. I will not shy away from the sword. I will not stand still when the trumpet sounds." —inspired by Job 39:22–24
  - I am fight ready.
  - I steal inches.
  - I don't flinch.
  - I show love.

- **Application:** Thankful List
  - Who am I particularly thankful for today?
  - What is something that happened yesterday that I'm thankful for?
  - What is something I am looking forward to today?
- **Application:** Prayer List
  - Who within my reach needs to be lifted up today?
- **Application:** Story List
  - What happened yesterday that is story-worthy?

Through this practice, over time, I have noticed an increase in my awareness of and intentionality with my values. Throughout the day, I find myself earmarking events to include as a story in my journal the next morning. In moments of adversity, I am reminded to tell myself to be fight ready. I've faithfully followed this morning ritual for about five years now, and it has had as big an impact on my ability to remain focused on my internal scoreboard as anything I have done.

Failure is a reality we all face, often numerous times each day. Yet we repeatedly neglect to establish a plan to handle it. With a plan in place, we are so much better able to navigate our emotions and quickly return to the present, best version of ourselves. Of course, a plan to recover from adversity is only as effective as our ability to execute it. Here are a few helpful exercises.

—————————— TAKE ACTION ——————————

Exercise: Failure-Recovery System

Why: To respond better to adversity

How: What do you do following a mistake? Create a physical routine to own it, move on, and get present. (Example: take a deep breath, say sorry, use your mantras.)

Exercise: Create Your Bookends

Why: To build energy into your day

How: Create a morning routine to help regulate your life. If you already have a routine, reflect on it to pinpoint what is and isn't beneficial for you. Identify three to five actions you will commit to every morning to start your day. Identify three to five actions you will commit to every evening to finish your day.

CHAPTER 12

The Process

If you quit on the process, you are quitting on the result.

—Idowu Koyenikan

In their book *Art & Fear*, authors David Bayles and Ted Orland tell a parable about the payoff of repeated practice. A pottery teacher split his class into two groups. The quality group was assigned to build the one best possible pot they could over the course of thirty days. The quantity group was assigned to produce one pot every day for thirty days. At the end of the thirty days, judges selected the best pots. Every one of the top pots came from the quantity group. The quality group had focused its efforts on creating one perfect pot. They thought a lot about how to do it, talked it through, and eventually built a nice, serviceable pot. The quantity group just kept making pots over and over. And with each pot they made, they learned what was good about their work and what wasn't. They then applied that learning into making the next pot.

It turns out this parable is based in fact . . . sort of. In writing what would become his first *New York Times* bestseller, *Atomic Habits*, James Clear reached out to the authors of *Art & Fear* to find out more about this ceramics lesson. In their emailed response, Bayles and Orland confirmed that, "Yes, the 'ceramics story' in *Art & Fear* is indeed true, allowing for some literary license in the retelling."[1] The real-world source of the parable was Jerry Uelsmann, a professor of film photography at the University of Florida. The authors retold the story using pottery because, in their words, "[We] are both photographers ourselves, and at the time we were consciously trying to broaden the range of media being referenced in the text."

Uelsmann had actually divided his classroom of photography students right down the center into two groups: the grade of those on the left side of the room would be based on the volume of their photographic production, with an output of one hundred photos earning an "A." Nothing about that grade would hinge on the substantive merit of the work they produced. Uelsmann's grading of the other half of the class was based on the quality of the image. "They would only need to produce one photo during the semester, but to get an A, it had to be a nearly perfect image." According to Clear's telling, not only did the best-quality photos come from the high-quantity/quality-irrelevant group, but the result also surprised even Uelsmann himself. Despite being free from worry about the quality of their output, the quantity-side students *learned from doing the work*.

Quantity leads to quality. We need to get going to get good. As Wilbur Wright said in the process of building the first-ever flying machine, "If you are looking for perfect safety, you will do well to sit on a fence and watch the birds; but if you really wish to learn, you must mount a machine and become acquainted with its tricks by actual trial."[2]

ATTENTION TO DETAIL

From 2014 to 2021, the Mercedes-AMG Petronas team (the "Silver Arrows") of Formula 1 racing won eight straight team championships. During that stretch, Mercedes won 111 Grand Prix races, an absurd 69 percent winning percentage. That string of unparalleled winning coincided with Toto Wolff's arrival in 2013 as an investor and executive.

"Wolff is a self-admitted stickler for even the smallest details,"[3] points out Anita Elberse, professor of business administration at Harvard Business School, in the *Harvard Business Review*. "A bit of a maniac" is how one competitor described Wolff's fanatical obsession with details. During his first visit to the Mercedes team factory months before the 2013 season started, Wolff was seated in the lobby waiting to meet the team principal, F1 legend Ross Brawn. "On the table were a crumpled *Daily Mail* newspaper from the week before and two old paper coffee cups," Wolff recalled to Elberse.[4] "I went up to the office to meet him, and at the end of our conversation I said, 'I look forward to working together. But just one thing—that reception area doesn't say 'F1,' and that's where it needs to start if we want to win.'"

Brawn, who had captained Scuderia Ferrari to many championships in the 2000s and had even led his own F1 team, Brawn GP, to the 2009 championship, begged to differ. "That doesn't make the car quicker," he said.[5] Wolff, having not yet accomplished anything in Formula 1, replied firmly, drawing from his principles, "For me it does. Because it means a sense for the detail." Upon taking over the job of team principal from Brawn the following year, Wolff led Mercedes to obsess about *all* the details, and the results followed.

No part of the team's operation is immune to Wolff's scrutiny. For an organization of nearly two thousand, it is hard to fathom its chief executive taking an active hand in how the bathrooms are cleaned, but that is exactly what Wolff does. He took notice the first time he used one of the bathrooms in the team's race weekend hospitality area. "It was dirty," he said, "and I thought, 'That cannot be. This is our home on a race weekend and where our sponsors come with their families.'" So, Wolff hired Miguel Guerreiro, a full-time "hygiene manager," whose job it would be to maintain the team's bathroom facilities to the same standard of excellence that Wolff expected of his engineers off the track and his drivers on it. "I physically showed him how I wanted him to clean the toilet, how to put the brush back, how to wipe the floor, how to put the soap bottles with the front facing forward, how to sanitize the handles, and so on. And I walked him through what I wanted his schedule for the week to be, and how on Sundays, when it is busy, I want him to park himself right next to the bathroom and make sure it is spotless after every guest."[6] When a reporter with the New Yorker found this hard to believe, Wolff halted their interview and called Guerreiro over.

"Miguel, can I steal thirty seconds of your time?" Wolff asked. "What did we discuss yesterday?"

"Exactly how the toilets were functioning and how we could improve because—" answered Guerreiro.

"We discussed about the soap—that you can't really reach it well. You don't know where the sensor is."

"Yes," Guerreiro said. "And the paper, you can't really see it."[7]

Some might argue that Wolff is a micromanager and wonder why he spends so much time on things that seemingly have nothing to do with horsepower, aerodynamics, or lap times. Wolff is aware. "Everybody laughed about us at the beginning," he said of his and Guerreiro's teamwork over latrine sanitation. "The point," he said, "is that I want to set the standards in what I do."[8] Wolff is sending a vividly clear message to his team. No job is too small. No detail is insignificant. Every member of the team plays a role in the excellence of Mercedes's team performance.

MAKE PRACTICE HARDER THAN THE GAMES

JJ Redick played fifteen seasons in the NBA after a storied career at Duke University. As a collegian, Redick was a consensus All American twice and named the National College Player of the Year in 2006. He's known as one of the best "pure shooters" to ever play basketball.

Of course, Redick was born with talent, but something more than raw talent made him into the world-class shooter he was throughout his career: *a love of the process.* During an appearance with former NBA contemporaries Quentin Richardson and Darius Miles on their podcast, *Knuckleheads*, Redick described his process for approaching his craft both during the season and in the offseason.

My offseasons were harder than the season. My offseasons were six days a week, two or three workouts a day. Saturdays off, Sundays make 342 shots exactly, every Sunday in the offseason for the last thirteen years. Why 342?

It's very simple. There are seven spots on the floor: twenty spot twos, twenty spot threes, three dribbles going right, three dribbles going left, plus twenty free throws. That's 342. Then I started cold tubbing, and they (the team trainers) wanted me to cold tub for twelve minutes. So, I'd cold tub for twelve minutes. And then I'd get to the point where I'd be like, "If I start my timer a little too early, I'm not going to get that full twelve minutes. I don't want to cheat myself." So, I started cold tubbing for twelve minutes and twenty-five seconds. Just to give myself some wiggle room, right?

[For] my routine on a normal game day, I knew exactly what I was going to eat for breakfast. I knew exactly when I was going to get to the gym. I knew exactly how many minutes I was going to spend in the hot tub before I went to the training table, then I got my work in the weight room for activation, then I got my pre-shootaround shooting, then my post-shootaround shooting, then my cold tub. I knew exactly what I was going to eat for lunch. Then I knew exactly when I was going to nap. I had my naps timed out, bro. By the end of my career, if I said, "I need to fall asleep at 1:05 to wake up at 3:30," I could do it like that. The whole day was planned out.

And my offseasons? If we lost (in the playoffs) on Saturday, I was in the gym on Monday. I loved the process. I loved everything that went into it.[9]

Was Redick born with athletic gifts? No doubt. Would those gifts alone have been enough to play fifteen years in the NBA? Doubtful. He built a system: a process unique to him that he knew he needed to do every day to be ready to go when the game started. We can all create our own process; excellence demands that we do. The results take care of themselves when we focus on what we actually do each day—not a faraway goal or ambition. No, it's what we do right now and the next day—and so on.

Redick's love for the process shouldn't surprise us. He was excellent, and that's what excellent people do. Was his career worthy of the Hall of Fame? He was a great shooter, but not many would say he's a Hall of Famer. But he didn't need to be. Excellence doesn't require you to be the best. It requires you to be *your* best. Redick may have been aware of other great players and shooters who were playing with him or who came before him, but his process wasn't concerned with that. His process was all about him becoming the best version of himself that he could possibly be.

Redick was meticulous with the details and obsessive about the routine, proof that he had committed to excellence long before this process and routine were in place. The process flowed from his love of progress. It's progress that excellence desires, not results. The process he built and committed to ensured that progress.

PROCESS-BASED GOALS VERSUS RESULTS-BASED GOALS

A mindset focused on results is the norm. The outcome is paramount in our society; hence, it becomes the priority in our mind. The typical way to set goals is to use the result we seek as our metric for success. Results such as a championship, promotion, or dream home are all very tangible, result-centered goals. And while the destination may be clear, the path to it is not.

Every NFL team wants to win the Super Bowl. Setting that as a goal is not the reason that the team that ultimately wins does. They win the Super Bowl because of their consistent work, day in and day out, and their ability to strive to get better, do the little things each day, focus on their fundamentals, be overprepared for each day and each game, and bounce back when things don't go their way. Their system for showing up each day, committed to their process, is what ultimately leads to victory.

The difficulty with merely identifying the result you aspire to is that it provides no guidance on how to accomplish it. Not only that, but research has also shown that results-based goals can be worse than ineffective. After reviewing various studies on results-based goal setting conducted in numerous countries and contexts, researchers from the business schools of Harvard University, Northwestern University, the University of Pennsylvania, and the University of Arizona argued that the beneficial effects of goal setting have been overstated and that systematic harm caused by goal setting has been largely ignored. In fact, results-focused goals can bring a variety of negative side effects, such as a rise in unethical behavior, a reduction in intrinsic motivation, a decrease in cooperation, and an increase in irrational risk-taking. Because of this, the study's authors proposed that "experts need to conceptualize goal setting as a prescription-strength medication that requires careful dosing, consideration of harmful side effects, and close supervision."[10]

Although we are told that the never-ending chase for the next result is the only way to achieve success, it's simply not true. The incessant pursuit of the next win will eventually leave us with one simple question: "Is that all there is?" The answer, of course, is no.

Herein lies the beauty of a process-oriented goal. Considering the outcome we desire, we are in the perfect position to uncover the root action that will give us the best chance to achieve what we aspire to. A process-oriented goal is a behavior. It's something we do, not something we get. After all, aren't all results the byproduct of the actions leading up to them? By setting goals focused on the process, we expend our energy on what's in our control. Though not guaranteed, a concentration on those specific behaviors has the best potential to lead us to our desired result.

This redirection of our focus from results to processes requires more than a simple commitment to process. It is vital that we completely surrender the outcome, giving up any result, good or bad. We like to tell ourselves that we have control of the outcomes, but we don't. It's nothing but an illusion society sells us. We don't control to whom the boss will grant the promotion. We can only control our behaviors, the process, how we go about doing the work. So, why not focus our goal on the controllable process rather than a result?

BC: On our team, our goals are process based ("What are we going to do on a day-to-day basis?") as opposed to results based ("Win the state championship"). As we are setting our goal in the preseason, I pose the following scenario to our team: imagine a ten-year-old boy and his dad are sitting in the stands watching our team play. After the game, what do you want them to say about our team?

This simple framework always elicits similar answers from our players. They'll say, "We want them to say that we play hard, we care about each other, we love the game, we're tough, we're smart." In order to create some consistency, we narrow that list down to three or four characteristics that are most important to our players that season. Next, we ask the question that ultimately provides us with our goal for the season: "What do we need to do on a daily basis to make those aspirational qualities a reality?"

It's one thing to *want* people to say we really care about each other. It's completely different to consistently *behave* in a way that makes our care for each other apparent to anyone watching us play. The daily behaviors we identify are our process as well as the goal we set for the season.

With the behaviors clearly identified, our coaches now have a consistent standard by which to operate. As I previously mentioned, in the 2020–2021 season, our goal was to "Attack every opportunity with purpose." Given that goal, our mindset was that it didn't matter whether we were doing routine drills in our gym or squaring off against the number-one team in the country; if an opportunity was presented, we attacked it with purpose. The trust was never in the result we hoped for; it was in that consistently behaving in this manner would propel us to be our best. With the outcome surrendered, we were free to attack opportunities, which led to more growth and development than the pursuit of any single result ever could.

In fact, the power of the process is seen in an experience many of us have when we reach big milestones of achievement. You finally accomplish this goal you thought was so grand—a graduation, a promotion, a raise—and once you're there, you're like, "Is this it? Is that all there is?" Regardless of the magnitude of the accomplishment, the feeling of satisfaction is fleeting. Why? It's simple: fulfillment is found in the process, not the result. The night we won the state championship, I was happy, of course. But it went away pretty quickly. The feeling of satisfaction and pride in the *arrival* is not as impactful as you might think.

RH: I can relate to that because I never envisioned publishing a book, let alone two or more. When it's over, you start thinking about the next one. Or I think about the process it took to do it because it's not about getting it done; it's about what I learned and the person I became while doing this hard thing. It really is about who you become while preparing for those moments. The reward for producing great work is the opportunity to keep doing it.

Shifting your focus to your inner scoreboard leads to a more fulfilling life. Whether you win the game or write a *New York Times* bestseller isn't fully within your control, but you can control your dedication to getting better each day. You can control how you choose to live your values. You can control the input you bring to the task. Outside influences and circumstances beyond your control have their own inputs, and the output is a combination of them all. Sometimes it will go your way, and sometimes it won't. In our experience, though, it seems that the people who are committed to their process each and every day seem to have it go their way more often than those who don't.

TAKE ACTION

Exercise: Process Goals

Why: To gain clarity on what's important

How: What characteristics and behaviors will maximize your chance to be your best? What will most likely keep you from performing at your best? Identify the two to three most important attributes you want to display. What must you do on a daily basis for those two to three characteristics to become the reality of who you are?

Exercise: The Little Things Are the Big Things

Why: To value the details

How: Consider your last great accomplishment, something you were very proud of. Make a list of twenty things that you did for that single accomplishment to happen.

CHAPTER 13

You Aren't as Tough
as You Could Be

*"Everyone is a bit scared," said the horse. "But we are less
scared together."*

—*The Boy, the Mole, the Fox and the Horse*
by Charlie Mackesy

RH: **Years ago, my dad was leading a thousand-person salesforce.**
His boss was a man named Bob Romeo. Romeo, who is now the
CEO of Anaqua (an intellectual-property software company), was
known for being tough, demanding, and having high expectations. He
came across as intimidating to people who didn't know him well.

My dad told me a story about the relationship he had built with
Romeo and how their level of trust enabled them to make decisions
quickly.

The real-estate people from our company called me to say they wanted to close our Boston office for cost savings. They said they couldn't get ahold of Bob Romeo and asked if I would speak with him. I called him and told him what was going on, and he asked me, "What do you think?" I replied that I thought it was a bad idea that would bring other unnecessary costs into our business as well as harm our sales performance. He agreed and told me to tell the real-estate person no.

We talked for about ten minutes. I called [the real-estate managers] back fifteen minutes after they called me and told them that we did not want to close Boston, per Bob's decision. The real-estate guy said, "How did you guys decide so quickly?" I replied, "Because we trust each other." When there is trust in the organization, things get done fast. There is minimal need to waste time "checking" or looking over trusted employees' shoulders. You listen to their reasoning and experiences and go with their decision in many or most cases.

When I asked Romeo how he came to trust my dad so quickly, he said, "He had a great reputation before I met him, and I felt that even more after working with him. There are many more stories like the Boston office one I could tell you about."

As my dad's experience shows, when trust is built, activated, and relied on, speed of action is a result. "Trust decreases transaction costs" is how retired four-star general Stanley McChrystal put it during his appearance on *The Learning Leader Show*.[1] When trust is involved, everything goes faster: decisions get made more quickly, meetings run shorter, and there is no need for meetings in between the meetings to figure out what people really think.

Warren Buffett once told the story of how his company, Berkshire Hathaway, wanted to acquire McLane from Walmart. McLane was a subsidiary of Walmart that generated $23 billion in sales, so it was a big deal. Here's how Buffett described it: "To make the McLane deal, I had a single meeting of about two hours with Tom Schoewe, [Walmart's] CFO, and we then shook hands. (He did, however, first call Benton-ville). Twenty-nine days later [Walmart] had its money. We did no 'due diligence.' We knew everything would be exactly as [Walmart] said it would be—and it was."[2]

For most companies, a deal of this size might take a year (or longer) to get done. Buffett has built a reputation for leading with trust and only working with others who do the same. Because of that, he acquired a $23 billion–dollar company in twenty-nine days. When you lead with skepticism or a cynical view of the world, you attract other cynics and repel trusting leaders. You can still get things done that way, but it will cost a lot more in time, money, and stress. As Stephen Covey, author of *The Speed of Trust*, wrote, "As trust goes up, speed goes up and cost goes down; as trust goes down, speed goes down and cost goes up."[3]

But the value of trust is more than simply being a decision acceler-ant. Paul Zak is a professor of economic sciences, psychology, and man-agement at Claremont Graduate University in Los Angeles, California, where he also serves as the founding director for the school's Center for Neuroeconomics Studies. In the course of his research, Zak used both survey data and measured brain activity during periods of work to examine the effect of trust on people and the work they do.

The differences between people's work experience in high-trust and low-trust organizations are striking. The people working within high-trust environments have:[4]

- Seventy-four percent less stress
- Fifty percent higher productivity
- Thirteen percent fewer sick days
- Seventy-six percent more engagement
- Twenty-nine percent more satisfaction with their lives
- Forty percent less burnout

These are real, tangible, and substantial benefits from an elevation in the level of trust. Trust means belief uncompromised by doubt. In the workplace, people can't do their best work if they doubt others' intentions or capabilities, the direction or viability of the organization, or, most importantly, their own ability to keep up with the demands placed on them.

VULNERABILITY IS THE ONLY PATH TO TRUE TRUST

There is no safe, risk-free path to building trust. That means operating without a backstop, contingency plan, or escape route in the event that things don't work out as planned. Holding something back in order to protect yourself in case of failure may be prudent, but it isn't trusting. In other words, to trust means to be vulnerable.

Vulnerability is the only path to true trust. There has been a misconception that equates vulnerability with weakness—Brook's high-school boys certainly believe that—but that couldn't be further from the truth. Author Brené Brown defines vulnerability as "having the courage to show up and be seen when we have no control over the outcome. Vulnerability is not weakness; it's our greatest measure of courage."[5] Brook's goal is that by the end of the year, the young men he coaches realize the strength in vulnerability and its power to build a team.

Without vulnerability, a team has no shot of reaching its potential. None of the exercises in building self-awareness or truth-sharing moments we talked about in earlier chapters can happen among people who cannot be vulnerable with each other.

You have to make a lot of investments in the trust account to cover just a single withdrawal. If you're willing to show your shortcomings and scars, talk about them, and let others into that vulnerability loop, then they feel like they can reciprocate and share theirs. That's how teams grow. Until you build trust with your team through vulnerability, you'll only be a fraction of what you're truly capable of being.

The best way to do this is for the leader to model the behavior. As a leader, show your cards when difficult things happen and you have a chance to strike back or say something about someone. If you choose not to and instead show kindness, you pull your people in closer. They'll know that if you're going to be kind to someone who doesn't necessarily deserve it, you will probably be kind to them, too. It creates a different environment.

This behavior is contagious. As they develop new patterns with each other, that habit of kindness ripples into their personal lives. Leading others to trust first is a leadership principle that has an impact deeper than we can possibly know. That is transformational leadership.

TRANSFORMATIONAL VERSUS TRANSACTIONAL LEADERSHIP

You can think of transactional and transformational approaches as sitting at two ends of a leadership continuum. On one side is transactional leadership, which requires simple management and direct authority. Little needs to be known about those we lead; what's required is direction and unrelenting pursuit. Results can be, and often are, obtained in this way.

On the other end of the spectrum lies transformational leadership. This approach requires trust and buy-in from those we lead. Deep relationships shatter the hierarchy of the transactional leadership model. Transformational leadership is contingent on knowing yourself, which allows you to fully know others.

Transactional Approach

A transactional person is someone who conceptualizes the majority of their actions within an exchange framework. It's like going through a drive-through: you give me my fries, I give you my money, and we're done. We both get what we want. Once the exchange is complete, the transactional relationship is over.

There are certainly times when this is an effective framework to use, but many people operate this way their entire lives. You can certainly set up your life as a series of transactions in which you are always asking yourself, "What can I get from that person?" and "What do I have to do to get it?" You might not even realize that you're doing it. It just becomes a default setting. In our consumer-driven, fast-paced society, it's an easy default posture to fall into.

But it's not the best way to connect with people meaningfully or to support their growth and development. Let's face it: that's not what we want from the majority of our interactions. We want to build deep, long-lasting relationships.

And our health and livelihood depend on it. According to Dr. Robert Waldinger, director of Harvard University's Grant and Glueck studies (a seventy-five-year longitudinal study that followed 268 Harvard men and a second cohort that followed 456 disadvantaged nondelinquent inner-city youths), "Our relationships and how happy we are in our relationships has a powerful influence on our health."[6] It is a conclusion that, in Dr. Waldinger's words, was a "surprising finding." "The people who were the most satisfied in their relationships at age fifty were the healthiest at age eighty," he says. Meaningful connections "protect people from life's discontents, help to delay mental and physical decline, and are better predictors of long and happy lives than social class, IQ, or even genes." This finding was as true for the group of men living in inner-city Boston as it was for those enrolled at Harvard University.

Transformational Approach

A transformational framework views interactions through the perspective of a relationship. If we are entering into a relationship together, even a minor one, I will be changed by it in some way, and you will, too. We will be transformed into something we weren't before. By definition, transformational friends change you. Transformational people carry a desire to be a value-adding resource to someone else. In leading, teaching, coaching, and so on, the hope is that people are different after having interacted with you. Do you aspire to be transformational? Do the people you lead change for the better because you are in a relationship with them?

RH: During my time playing quarterback at Miami University, I had to learn that I did not give the team as good a chance to win as did the other quarterback, Ben Roethlisberger. The reality was that I didn't add enough value to the lives of the coaching staff and to my teammates. Now, if I want to be a part of someone's life and I'm not adding value, I ask myself, "Why do I deserve to be in their life?" I try to think that way with all my interpersonal relationships. How am I adding value and facilitating positive transformation? If I'm not doing that, then I don't deserve to reap the benefits of those relationships. If my default setting is always thinking of ways to positively impact people and leave them better, over time, I'm probably going to build great relationships.

Which brings us back to the topic of this chapter: trust. In transactional relationships, trust isn't necessary. In an exchange, you get what you pay for, and you pay for what you get. In more complex exchanges, we use contracts to precisely document the rights and obligations of each party so neither side has to take the risk of just trusting the other to do right by them. But if your goal is to generate a web of trust that connects you to your team and the people on your team to each other, then set your sights on the transformational side of the leadership continuum. Lead from there first, and watch the blossoming of trust that follows.

Apart from embracing the vulnerability that comes with showing trust first, here are three concrete actions you can take to go further in showing that you are a trustworthy guide to the people you lead.

Become More Reasonable

RH: During a given week, I might interview three or four leaders from a wide array of job functions, industries, and geographic locations. Doing this forces me to open my mind to different points of view, sets of life experiences, and ways people view the world. I try to be a good listener. I try to be curious. I try to learn something new from every conversation. Doing this has made me more reasonable over time. Reading increases my knowledge, but it's speaking with people with a sincerity to hear and understand them that increases my tendency to be fair and sensible. I live more in the gray and less in the black-and-white because of this.

This is something author Polina Pompliano talked with me about when we recorded a podcast together. Since 2017, Pompliano has been writing long-form profiles of the people and companies she finds most interesting. Here's what she said:

> If there's one thing you can do right now to improve both your personal and professional life, it's this: eliminate absolute statements from your vocabulary. Absolute statements are those that assume an idea or a statement is absolutely, undeniably, 100 percent true. Words like "everyone," "no one," "never," "always." This type of all-or-nothing thinking tells me two things: one, you perceive life events in an emotional way, and two, your worldview is likely distorted because you don't see nuance.

I know because I was this person. It's through interviewing and studying so many different types of people that my mind has opened to the idea that the world is not black and white. It's not either/or. It's not this or that. Most situations allow you to wedge in a tiny bit of nuance.[7]

To better understand the nuances of life, it's helpful to expose yourself to people with different viewpoints from your own. And instead of approaching them with judgment, be curious. When I find myself becoming judgmental about a person, I think of what Abraham Lincoln said: "I don't like that man. I must get to know him better." Judgment closes the door to curiosity, and curiosity is a fundamental element to excellent leadership. Each person is unique based on their specific set of life experiences. It's worth approaching them with an open mind and a desire to learn both about them and from them. As my friend Larry Seiler says, "Treat everyone as your mentor." You never know what you might learn.

This reasonableness creates the social space for trust to grow. Tim Urban wrote a book titled *What's Our Problem?* It includes the concept of being a "high-rung thinker." High-rung thinking is a mindset that values truth above all else. It prioritizes productive and independent thinking, which allows for the revision or rejection of ideas (i.e., changing your mind). This mindset is humble, self-aware, and free of bias. In high-rung thinking, hypotheses are formed from the bottom up, following evidence wherever it leads, with a default position of "I don't know" on any given topic. When others know that your mind is open to learning from a wide range of perspectives and you're open to updating your view on a topic when better evidence presents itself, they realize you're more trustworthy. Why? Because they know your only desire is to find the truth, and that makes you a safe person who can be told that you may be wrong. When people know that about you, they are more willing to take the risk of vulnerability with you. Trust grows as a result.

BC: As I've matured and grown as a teacher and coach, I've realized the value in the input of our players. Many times, the best answers in a crucial moment of the game can be found within those in the arena playing the game. Rather than dictate and demand during timeout, I am now more likely to simply ask our players what they see or what they want to do. Of course, I have the final say and can agree or go in another direction if I deem it necessary, but more often than not they're right. And, if they believe in it enough to share it with the group, "right" may be irrelevant. It's more about what they believe in. Their reason is king in those moments.

AAU basketball is another example that demonstrates the importance of practicing extra reason. The Amateur Athletic Union (AAU) is the foundation for grassroots basketball and often gets a bad reputation in the coaching world for a lack of fundamentals, selfish play, and a focus on highlights over solid team play. Most will acknowledge this truth. However, there is much more to the story and to ignore the positives accompanying AAU basketball is unreasonable. The competition is typically very good, the exposure to higher levels and different types of players is exceptional, and the relationships that are built will often last a lifetime. As with anything, AAU is neither good nor bad. It's how we use it that makes it so.

Be On Time

RH: One of the small details that is often overlooked is punctuality. I am amazed at how common it is to be late to meetings. It's even worse when leaders perpetuate the notion that it's acceptable by conceding, "We'll wait a few minutes for everyone to get here." *No.* Start the meeting when it's supposed to start, regardless of how many people are there. They will learn that your meetings are different. If they want all the information, then they need to be on time. There is no repeating of directions for the people who are late. I've learned this over the course of many years, and the leaders who are part of my meetings have as well.

Now, some may be recoiling at this and think it is a bit harsh. Typically, when I share this with people who work in the corporate world, I get lots of eye rolls and "You don't understand" comments. Maybe I don't and I'm out of touch with how normal it is to disrespect others and be late to meetings (or, worse, to start them late). But let me explain why I think this criticism misses the mark.

My dad always says, "Honor the present." By this, he means to honor the people who did it right by not making them wait. There will always be excuses for why people are late. "Oh, I was in back-to-back meetings and my last meeting went overtime." Whatever the excuse, your tardiness sends one message to everyone else: "My time is more important than yours. I'm not willing to sacrifice my time for our time." Tardiness expresses arrogance and selfishness.

How about we do it differently? Let's be on time. Let's honor the present. Does a life event happen every once in a while and cause us to miss a meeting or be late because our child missed the bus and we drove them to school? Of course. But those are exceptions. I'm talking about a leader who is known to always be late. Don't be that person. Be the leader who is always on time. It is a tangible way to demonstrate your trustworthiness to your team: you are where you are supposed to be when you are supposed to be there.

BC: Like most coaches, punctuality is a habit that is anything but a detail. We have a program-wide policy that everyone should be dressed and ready a minimum of fifteen minutes before the start of practice. Players should not be sitting in the locker room with their sweats on, leaning back on their lockers checking their phones, or walking around with their shoes untied. The expectation, and standard, is dressed and ready. To quote legendary University of Michigan football coach Bo Schembechler, "Early is on time, and on time is late."

Be Consistent

RH: In December 2021, I was at the Baha Mar Resort in the Bahamas on a trip to celebrate the top performers from Insight Global. At the opening-night cocktail reception, a young woman approached me and said, "I love how you and Brook design my learning for me each week." Somewhat surprised, I asked, "What do you mean?"

"On Monday mornings I listen to your podcast, and on Thursday afternoons I read Coach Cupps's new blog post. I've done that each week for the past year, and you guys have helped me so much." She further explained, "I love knowing that you both will have something new and interesting for me every week."

Apart from her appreciation for our content, there's something else going on in her words that I want to highlight. Read her words again.

"each week"
"every week"

One of the most effective ways to build trust with someone is to consistently show up for them. Leave no doubt that you will be there and add value to their life. When that happens over and over for weeks/months/years, deep trust is built. When you do something like publish at the same time every week, no matter what, that consistency enables others to build a routine they can rely on without worrying that it will be disrupted. That trust allows them to focus their decision and planning efforts on so many other things in life that are unpredictable and inconsistent.

Over the course of my younger brother's playing career with the Green Bay Packers, I developed friendships with many of his teammates. In the quieter moments when AJ wasn't around, I would ask them what they valued most about him as a teammate. As his brother, I was (and still am) so proud of him, so I often looked for opportunities to hear cool stories about him. The responses were remarkably consistent. They all said things like: "I know he will always be where he's supposed to be." "I never worry for a second that he won't be in his gap, call the right defense, make the right check at the line, and get us in the best position to do well. That's just what he does."

Or they talked about his preparation: "I see him finishing up his extra weight-room session every morning as I'm walking into the facility. I know that dude is going to be ready on Sunday." In fact, Andrew Brandt, the team's former vice president, told me a funny story about AJ's obsession with preparation: "AJ is the only guy I can remember in the history of signing a rookie contract that came directly from the weight room, dripping in sweat, signed it immediately, and went right back to the weight room to finish his workout before practice that day."[8]

All those actions built deep trust of AJ in his teammates. Words like *reliable*, *dependable*, and *prepared* are not the sexiest terms. However, they are the bedrock of consistency, and consistency equals trust. This can manifest in many ways. Walking your seven-year-old to the bus stop every morning builds trust. Being on time and prepared for your Monday morning meeting builds trust. Sending your team a consistent post-meeting recap email every time builds trust. Showing up consistently for the people you lead is one of the most effective ways to build trust.

BC: Consistency is one of the primary messages we attempt to convey at our preseason retreat. For the past twelve years, each player at the retreat has chopped down a tree. Most of our players have never held an axe, much less used one to chop down a dead tree in the middle of the woods.

All of our players approach it in different ways. The guys who have played baseball rear back and take huge hacks, attempting to demonstrate their beautiful home-run swing that's sure to knock the tree over in just a few swings. We have the smart guys who carefully negotiate for the sharpest axe then calculate every swing to be sure they're striking the tree in just the right spot. And we usually end up with at least one guy who's so uncomfortable with the axe in his hands that he chokes halfway up the handle to ensure more control, lightening the blows but doubling the frequency.

The best part of the whole experience is that they all end up in the same place. After about ten minutes of constant swinging, shedding a layer of clothing, adjusting their strategy a few times, and making virtually no significant progress, they all begin looking around at their coaches and teammates. And they all ask the same question: "What do I do now?"

The answer, though clear, is not what they want to hear: keep swinging.

If we are willing to take an in-depth look at excellence, in ourselves and others, what we will realize is that every single area of excellence was founded on consistency. Some may start further ahead than others, but consistency is required regardless. There are no exceptions.

——————————— TAKE ACTION ———————————

Exercise: Same Station

Why: To appreciate the need for a common goal

How: Ask everyone on your team to pick their favorite song on their phone, then play it at the same time. Allow a few minutes for everyone to appreciate the chaos. Now, give them three minutes to decide on a song to play together. Have them all start this song at the exact same time. Allow a few minutes to appreciate the music. Connect this to establishing a consistent goal the team is focused on. If everyone is chasing their own goal, it's chaos. In order to find

a common tune, everyone must be willing to share their thoughts and compromise their ideal personal choice for the good of the team.

Exercise: Show Me Love

Why: To live with gratitude

How: We all give and receive love and appreciation differently. None is right
or wrong. How does it make you feel when teammates show you love? Write
and share three ways your teammates can best show you love.

CHAPTER 14

We're All Role Players

You don't get harmony when everyone sings the same note.
—Doug Floyd

Jimmy Butler had just led his team, the Miami Heat, to the Eastern Conference championship in 2023, earning the MVP award for the series. Following that win, he was asked about some of the more unknown "role players" who had stepped up to help the team win. Butler responded, "I don't call them 'role players'; I call them 'teammates.' Your role can change any given day."[1]

We all have a role. Admittedly, some are more desirable than others. Everyone wants to be the star, right? Everyone wants to be the quarterback or the CEO. Too often, many aspire to these positions because they misunderstand the role.

The star of the movie has a role. The CEO of a company has a role. The quarterback of a football team has a role. The quarterback is not a lineman; blocking is not his job. He's not the kicker; making kicks is not his job. He's the quarterback. For his team to perform at its best, he has to stick to doing what a quarterback does: throwing the ball, calling plays, and reading the defense. These all fall within his realm of duty. However, what makes the quarterback's role unique is that the job doesn't end there. The quarterback is often held responsible for the overall performance of the team (it's the only position in football where a win/loss record is often added next to the quarterback's name). Part of his role is not only accepting this but welcoming it. It is a role that can only be done well if the person leans in and embraces all of it. Like many positions of leadership, quarterback is a role many people seek for its visibility and perceived glory while neglecting to consider the full responsibility the role represents.

Rather than viewing the duties of a role as a limiting parameter placed on us, we need to shift our perspective to one of acceptance and empowerment. Roles are precisely what allow us to best serve our team, tap into our greatest strengths, and maximize our potential. As leaders, our relationship with roles is even more significant because we become responsible for placing team members into roles that both capitalize on their strengths and serve the team.

In his book *The Hidden Life of Trees*, Peter Wohlleben writes about why trees need each other. His observation of their interdependence is worth quoting at length.

> A tree is not a forest. On its own, a tree cannot establish a consistent local climate. It is at the mercy of wind and weather. But together, many trees create an ecosystem that moderates extremes of heat and cold, stores a great deal of water, and generates a great deal of humidity. And in this protected environment, trees can live to be very old. To get to this point, the community must remain intact no matter what. If every tree were looking out only for itself, then quite a few of them would never reach old age. Regular fatalities would result in

many large gaps in tree canopy, which would make it easier for storms to get inside the forest and uproot more trees. The heat of summer would reach the forest floor and dry it out. Every tree would suffer.[2]

Wohlleben's insight serves as a powerful metaphor for how real teamwork works. Each role without the rest is like a tree without the forest. Each role serves the others, and within this system of interdependent connection, we realize that no role is more important than any other. There is no hierarchy of trees in a forest. Likewise, there is no hierarchy of roles on true teams.

DESTROY HIERARCHIES

Whether we are talking about people or wolves, the concept of "being the alpha" is a popular one. However, what it actually means in terms of behaviors and social structure is not settled science. In fact, it is a topic that is widely disputed. David Mech, senior research scientist at the US Geological Survey, has been studying the behavior of wolves since 1958. He believes that while the concept of *alpha* "connotes top ranking in some kind of hierarchy," the application of this term to wolves and wolf packs is misleading and that it "falsely [implies] a rigid, force-based dominance hierarchy."[3]

As far back as the 1940s, observers such as biologist Rudolph Schenkel have propounded the popular view that a pack of wolves involves several individual animals all "vying for dominance but held in check by the 'alpha' pair, the alpha male and the alpha female."[4] The problem is that this was based on observations of wolves in captivity rather than in their natural habitat. The importance of this difference goes beyond the environment because in nature, wolf packs are made up of family members. As Mech points out in his paper "Alpha Status, Dominance, and Division of Labor in Wolf Packs," the relationship of each wolf in the pack to each other is the better lens through which to interpret their behavior in the wild.

> Labeling a high-ranking wolf alpha emphasizes its rank in a dominance hierarchy. However, in natural wolf packs, the alpha male or female are merely the breeding animals, the parents of the pack, and dominance contests with other wolves are rare, if they exist at all. During my 13 summers observing the Ellesmere Island pack, I saw none.
>
> Thus, calling a wolf an alpha is usually no more appropriate than referring to a human parent or a doe deer as an alpha. Any parent is dominant to its young offspring, so "alpha" adds no information. Why not refer to an alpha female as the female parent, the breeding female, the matriarch, or simply the mother? Such a designation emphasizes not the animal's dominant status, which is trivial information, but its role as pack progenitor, which is critical information . . . Even the much-touted wolf dominance hierarchy is primarily a natural reflection of the age, sex, and reproductive structure of the group . . .[5]

The idea that wolves in a pack act cooperatively because of their family ties rather than as an act of submission to the social force of a dominant alpha is a striking difference from how we think wolves in packs act. Ironically, it turns out that domesticated dogs are the canids most dedicated to strong hierarchical behavior. Researchers from the University of Veterinary Medicine Vienna discovered this by using a variety of meal-focused tests on different socialized packs of both mixed-breed dogs and wolves. In one such test, they presented a single bowl of food to a pair of dogs from the same pack: a high-ranking and a low-ranking one. They did the same with matched pairs of wolves. Cooperation occurred among the wolves, as each ate at the same time as the other without issue. The dogs, on the other hand, were a different story: "At times, the more dominant wolves were 'mildly aggressive toward their subordinates, but a lower ranking dog won't even try . . . They don't dare to challenge.'"[6]

Why is that? The researchers had a theory, and it undercuts the long-standing idea that dogs and humans have a cooperative relationship based on breeding designed for that purpose: "It's not about having a common goal. It's about [dogs] being with us, but without conflict. We tell them something, and they obey." Because mankind bred domesticated dogs for "obedience and dependency," that has oriented dogs to think and operate within a hierarchical framework. Wolves, on the other hand, have never had a need to operate this way, so they do not.

Not only does this framework of dependence foster aggressive behavior aimed at hierarchical domination, but it also appears to inhibit traits like initiative and problem-solving. Dr. Monique Udell, director of the Human-Animal Interaction Laboratory at Oregon State University, presented both domestic dogs and captive wolves with the following test. Each animal received a sealed container holding pieces of summer sausage and was given two minutes to open it. Of the ten wolves, eight succeeded in getting it open and earning the sausage treat. Not a single one of the twenty dogs (ten pets and ten from local shelters) accomplished the task. Worse yet, *most did not even try.* To further test the hypothesis that dependence on humans was the issue, Dr. Udell tried the test with dog puppies. They succeeded just like the wolves, showing that "dogs are no less capable of the task than wolves, but 'as the dog grows and becomes more dependent on its human owner that [independent] behavior is inhibited," Dr. Udell reported.[7]

Hierarchy incentivizes competition and disincentivizes cooperation. As soon as people sense a hierarchy in their roles, the entire structure of cooperative teamwork falls apart. Team members immediately begin trying to move up the ranks in order to gain more power. The lack of a hierarchy removes this struggle, empowering everyone to flourish within their roles and taking the team's fortunes with them. Hierarchies also establish and perpetuate dependence. One of the most common phrases you will hear in a culture of hierarchy is, "That's not my job." In the view of team members, hierarchies match reward with responsibility, duty with position. If you don't do your job, then I can't do mine.

NO TEAM CAPTAINS

While we are on the subject of the duty of leaders to steward the narrative of a team's standards and culture, let us take a minute to examine the role of team captains. Coaches aren't responsible for the standards; neither are captains. Every single person on the team is responsible for upholding the standards and holding themselves and each other to them.

BC: I'm not averse to the concept of team captains. What I am averse to is the traditional method for selecting them. The most common approach is for team members to vote. Some programs use nominations from players or coaches to decide the voting options. Sometimes restrictions are placed on who can be nominated, such as limiting it to seniors or upperclassmen. Others will hold an open voting session without nominations. All of these approaches attempt to generate buy-in from team members through active participation in the process. Nothing is wrong with this line of thinking. The problem is with the idea that captains are required in the first place.

The best teams operate with little to no hierarchies among teammates. We believe that a player-led team is the best kind of team. And we think that by naming captains and expecting them to hold everyone accountable, we are creating a player-led team. That's not always the case. By placing a "C" on someone's chest, we could be installing a hierarchy. We are creating a captain-led team, which isn't much different than a coach-led team. If we want a team led by its members, we should expect everyone to be responsible for the standards of the team. All are important. All are needed to accomplish our goals. And all are responsible for the standards of the team.

If you want to know who the functional captains are, just stand back and watch. No one needs to be nominated, and no one needs to vote. The actions speak loudly enough. When you look back over the course of a season's body of work, the answer becomes obvious. So, that's what we do. Naming a captain following a season allows us to recognize the team member who best exemplified our standards and held others to them. Doing this before the season simply adds an unnecessary burden on a few individuals and creates the exact type of hierarchy we spend the season trying to eliminate.

STANDARD BEARERS

BC: Our Breakfast Club has become a staple of Centerville Basketball. The early morning workouts with your teammates provide much of the lifeblood of the program. Some days we will have as many as thirty players working on their game at 6 AM. But that wasn't always the case. It started with one: Joey Weingartner. Joey was the first player to believe in the Breakfast Club. For over a year, Joey worked out in the morning by himself. His faithfulness empowered others, years after him, to trust in that work. Some would consider him the Godfather of the Breakfast Club. We call him the standard bearer.

Regardless of your age or era, we all recognize standard bearers when we see them. Standard bearers embody what excellence looks like. They illustrate both hope and reality. We see it's possible, and we also see that we're not there yet. In addition to that, acknowledging someone as a standard bearer is incredibly empowering to that individual and often leads them to push the standard even higher.

To be clear, being the leader is not the same as being the standard bearer. In fact, the roles should *not* be the same. Standard bearers give leaders someone to point to so they can say, "Do it like they do it." This role is not limited to tangible, outcome-based examples that we can see and measure. We have standard bearers in all aspects of life, and often it's the ones who bear the standard for the process we want to reinforce that can have the most impact on our teams. We can have standard bearers for our core values, for handling adversity, for handling success, for serving others, for commitment to the team, and for bringing energy to the group.

You get the idea. Anything you value and think is important for your team to do well has a standard bearer. Identify your standard bearers in the areas you deem most important. Let them know that they are the model or standard others are aiming for. And notify the rest of the team that these are the people we should be watching and learning from.

One note of caution: the standard-bearer tag can become a means of comparison and unhealthy competition if not handled correctly. The mindset of those pursuing excellence will naturally bend toward a desire to be the standard bearer in all aspects of life. First, we must realize this is unrealistic, and second, we must embrace the pursuit of better—allowing those in front of us to push our standards ever higher.

Rapper, singer, and songwriter Kanye West described this embrace well when he differentiated between competition and rivalry when asked about Drake. In a Clique TV interview, West said, "I think anything has to be a competition. You know, I think healthy competition is better than rivalry. Rivalry becomes a cancer. It becomes like termites in your house. I think healthy competition is something where you appreciate how hard this person goes. You know, I think Michael [Jackson] needed Prince. Everybody needs somebody to kick their ass a little bit."[8] Healthy competition allows the standard bearer to lift everyone else to a higher standard.

DECISION-MAKERS

Too often, organizations operate as if decision-making belongs to leadership alone. This leads to a system where information flows in only one direction: toward those making the decisions. The result is an organization that can only act as fast as its internal communication systems can effectively move that information from where it is generated to where it is used.

We take it for granted that this is just how things work. But it doesn't have to be this way. In recent years, a chorus of leadership voices have risen to challenge this conventional paradigm. Two of our favorites are Kat Cole and Stanley McChrystal.

Cole's first job at Hooters was as a hostess, where her work ethic quickly made her stand out as a member of the frontline staff. After setting a record of twenty-two consecutive close opens (shifts where you close the restaurant late at night and are back at work to open it the next morning), she was asked to travel to Sydney, Australia, to open a new restaurant. By the age of twenty-six, Kat was a vice president with the company, working with colleagues who were twice her age and who had been in the business longer than she had been alive.

But even as she's ascended the corporate ranks to C-suite positions with companies like Cinnabon and now Athletic Greens, she has maintained her respect for the perspectives of those on the front lines of a business. "I learned early in my career that the strongest learning leaders stay incredibly close to the people closest to the action," Cole told

Ryan during a live podcast recording of *The Learning Leader Show* at the corporate headquarters of Insight Global in Atlanta. "Any humble human leader knows that the people closest to the action know the right thing to do in any situation long before the leader can take action. The problem with the team members closest to that action is that they lack the authority to do something about it."[9]

Fixing that lack of authority is at the heart of retired four-star general Stanley McChrystal's leadership message. After taking over the Joint Special Operations Command in 2003, during the darkest days of combat against a terroristic insurgency in Iraq, McChrystal implemented a new model for organizational teamwork he called "empowered execution." To facilitate this, he hosted ninety-minute daily briefings over a worldwide video link so that as many as 7,500 team members could hear the same information at the same time. Everyone from top-of-the-chain commanders to frontline soldiers and operators were all on the same page with regard to their operations, the intelligence that shaped them, and the challenges they faced.

What was radical about McChrystal's version of an all-hands call each day was neither the size of the gathering nor the daily cadence. Rather, it was the purpose: to equip those closest to the action with the information they needed to make the best decisions as quickly and nimbly as possible. As he says, "Battles are not won by generals, but by privates and sergeants on the frontlines."[10] And "if forces wait for information to travel all the way up the chain of command to the person in charge," he adds, "by the time the decision reaches the frontline force again, the decision could be wrong, outdated, or ill-informed." This is why McChrystal worked to make clear to his troops executing a mission that "if, when you get on the ground, the order we gave you is wrong, execute the order we should have given you" instead.[11]

By taking this approach, McChrystal successfully reshaped a slow, classically hierarchical organization that had been flailing against a decentralized foe into a nimble, networked "team of teams." In October 2003, when he took command of JSOC, its forces were conducting raids on al-Qaeda in Iraq at a rate of four per month. Three years later, JSOC's pace had accelerated by a factor of seventy-five to three hundred raids per month. The tide of the fight against the insurgency had shifted.

"Empowered execution" means pushing the decision-making authority down to where the information is rather than pushing the information up to where the decisions get made. In this model, the expectation and authority to make decisions and solve the problem lie with the people who are already well informed and close to the problem. It is those factors and not any particular role per se that defines who the decision-maker should be. In other words, being informed about the team's overall mission, goals, strategy, and challenges, as well as making the decisions necessary to solve the problem that sits in front of you, is everybody's responsibility on a team.

—————————— TAKE ACTION ——————————

Exercise: Role Identification

Why: To create clarity of your role

How: Identify two strengths and one weakness for yourself and each teammate. Share them with the group. From this, identify one primary role and two secondary roles for yourself on the team. Present these roles to the group, allowing for feedback or redirection.

Exercise: Team Debriefs

Why: To build trust, commitment, and accountability

How: In groups of four to six people, answer the following questions:

- What did I do well?
- What could I have done better?
- How will I fix it?
- Who performed well today?
- What did they do well?

Then, express love and gratitude for being part of the group.

CHAPTER 15

Push, Pull, or Drag

We can't inspire the best in others without a compelling reason that explains why they should care.

—Tanveer Naseer

A question all leaders must answer is whether the people they are leading are actually following them. This metric is a simple external scoreboard to determine whether a leader is leading or, as the old saying goes, just taking a walk. But there's a more interesting question that looks deeper—an internal score that looks at more than mere outcome. In fact, the answer to this question may indicate an underlying problem that the external score alone can't reveal.

The question is this: *Why* are they following?

RH: As I wrote in my first book, *Welcome to Management*, "Compliance can be commanded but commitment cannot."[1] If you're my boss, you can force me to do something until I no longer care about having the job, but as a leader, you can't force me to commit or be compelled.

You have to earn that every single day. Are you a leader that your people want to commit to?

As long as your leadership style is aimed at achieving compliance from your team, there will be a cap on what you can achieve. To be sure, you can get results with the "Hey, I'm your boss. Do it or find another job" approach. But in forcing compliance, you are forfeiting the benefits of tapping into the full potential of the people you lead. A team that follows because they're inspired and compelled by the leadership makes for a much more dynamic system. They want to bring all their knowledge, skills, and experience to bear rather than simply check a box.

If you lead people, you should be thinking about how you can inspire them to follow your vision rather than simply forcing them to. This requires you to hold up the mirror to yourself and ask, "Am I behaving in a way that would make someone want to commit to what we're doing?"

Some leaders roll their eyes at soft-skill topics such as kindness, trust, vulnerability, and accountability. "Why can't I be the senior leader and just stick to the facts, leaving all the personal stuff out of it? Can't I just get up in front of my people, present the numbers, and articulate our goal?" In other words, "Can't I just point to the external scoreboard? Why can't winning there be enough?"

You can. A lot of people do it that way, particularly if what they are hoping to win is a short-term, transactional situation. Commanding has a place in the story of leadership; it's just not the central theme. Safety matters, urgent time constraints, and work requiring a very specific series of actions are a few examples that lend themselves to a command approach. But you probably won't become a transformational leader this way. Your people won't be satisfied or innovative because you haven't built relationships of trust nor created a safe environment to do risk-taking work in.

BC: The first seven years of my coaching career, I subscribed to the theory that "If you can't compel, command." Needless to say, I could not compel anyone. Of course, "could not" isn't really the right choice of words. In reality, I did not want to invest the time and energy into compelling anyone.

I didn't even start with the idea of compelling. I became a high-school boys varsity basketball coach at the age of twenty-three. At that point, I thought *command* was synonymous with *coach*. So that's what I did. I directed. I rewarded. I punished. I told everyone in our program what to do, how to do it, and when to do it. I was clearly in charge. If you couldn't tell by watching me work, you could have asked, and I would have gladly told you who was the boss.

My command-and-demand approach led to reasonable results. Here in Ohio, where we play twenty regular-season games each year, our teams had years when we won as many as eighteen. By this external metric of coaching effectiveness, I was a success. I had decent, surface-level relationships with some of our players. Not so much with others. Some seasons we met our potential, and some seasons we didn't. I figured, "Such is life as a high-school basketball coach." While commanding, I always felt like our teams had a ceiling. We could only be as good as our talent allowed—and I was right. With my approach to leading, we did have a ceiling. But it wasn't a ceiling created by the talent of our players. It was one I had installed myself by the way I had chosen to lead.

After my seventh season, I had had enough. The emptiness of hollow victories provided no satisfaction or fulfillment. I was serving myself and no one else. I needed either to find another career or change my approach to it. That's when I decided to aim for more and made the transition from commanding our team to attempting to compel them. You can always command, while you must *try* to compel. It's not certain. Sometimes it works, sometimes it doesn't. Multiple efforts are required. The investment is much more significant, but the payoff is exponentially greater. Through this change in my approach to leading, Daniel Coyle's *Culture Code* equation became true: two plus two really did equal ten. There is no ceiling when those we lead are compelled.

The trajectory of our team's Breakfast Club through the years is probably the clearest proof of the payoff from leading this way. Breakfast Club, as you might recall from earlier, is the time before school when our players do individual and partner workouts to improve their skills. When I first started Breakfast Club over twenty years ago, I offered it as an option. Unsurprisingly, given that the players are just like most fifteen- to eighteen-year-olds, they chose not to attend. So I started making them attend. The results were as spotty as the players' compliance was begrudging.

When I switched my leadership focus to being compelling, I changed attendance at Breakfast Club back to optional, while painting a clearer image of what values and behaviors our program was aspiring to instill in each player. I connected their 6 AM commitment directly to our value of being passionate about whatever you choose to do. The number of players who attended initially dropped. But because those who showed up chose to be there, the quality of their work and development was significantly better. As they continued to attend, they became more and more engaged. Others witnessed this growth and began attending because they were compelled to do so, not because I had made them. We went from a single player attending Breakfast Club every morning to over thirty. Organic growth like this—both in the number of followers and in the effectiveness of their work—doesn't come from a command style of leadership.

Given the progress on our internal scoreboard, it is no surprise that external results followed as well. Our teams at two different schools have set school records for wins multiple times over. We've had winning streaks in the forties and won numerous championships. Of course, those achievements pale in comparison to the quality of the deep relationships we are now able to build with our players through the collaborative nature of compelling leadership.

"DON'T MESS WITH TEXAS"

In the mid-1980s, the state of Texas had a huge mess on its hands, and it was only getting bigger. The bill to clean up the trash tossed alongside the Texas highways was costing the state's department of transportation over $20 million annually and growing by about 17 percent a year. The fact that littering was already a criminal offense and carried a stiff fine didn't seem to matter. Relying on the public's forced compliance with the law was not a winning strategy against the rising tide of refuse sweeping across the Texas prairie landscape.

The problem with Texas's efforts to stop littering was all about focus. The message of anti-littering campaigns focused on concern for the environment, but according to market-research surveys, the Texans who were doing all the littering didn't care about that. As organizational storyteller Paul Smith said during his appearance on *The Learning Leading Show*, "It turned out what people in Texas really care about is *Texas*."[2]

With this insight, a clever campaign slogan was born. Recalling how his own mother would decry the state of his childhood bedroom—"This is just a mess!"—Tim McClure of Austin-based marketing agency GSD&M pitched an ad campaign centered on a new slogan. "We thought the way to get it into the public's consciousness quickest was to let Texans own it," McClure would later tell *Smithsonian Magazine*. Thus, the phrase "Don't mess with Texas" was born. "I don't think they would have put something that said, 'Don't litter Texas.' 'Don't trash our state.' I don't think they'd do it, but because it had that Texas bravado to it they adopted 'Don't mess with Texas' as their own battle cry."[3] Smith succinctly described this shift in perspective deployed by the Texas Department of Transportation: "They attached their problem to something that Texans did care about, because it turned out Texans didn't care about their problem."

On New Year's Day 1986, football fans from all over Texas and around the country tuned in to watch the fiftieth anniversary of a Dallas institution: the Cotton Bowl. The game is a college-football classic, best known for an improbable goal-line stand in which the Aggies of Texas A&M stuffed Auburn's Heisman Trophy–winning Bo Jackson and kept him out of the end zone on three straight plays from the one-yard line.

It was during this nationally televised event that Texas's new anti-littering campaign launched. The thirty-second commercial featured local blues icon Stevie Ray Vaughan picking out the tune to "I've Been Working on the Railroad" on his guitar while seated before a giant Texas state flag. In addition to laying out the scope of the litter problem and explaining that it was a crime, the voice-over narration also described it as "an insult to the Lone Star State." It ended with a close-up of Vaughn as he uttered the famous line, "Don't mess with Texas."[4]

The impact was immediate and dramatic. Within a single year, roadside litter had been reduced by 29 percent. The following year, it went down another 54 percent. By 1990, four years into the campaign, the amount of trash on the side of Texas highways was down a staggering 72 percent.

That is what a *compelling* message can do.

LEADING TO FOLLOW, FOLLOWING TO LEAD

On May 25, 2015, a pair of US Air Force F-15C fighter jets took off from Barnes ANG Base in Westfield, Massachusetts. The two planes of the 131st Fighter Squadron of the Massachusetts Air National Guard were scrambled to investigate a commercial airliner reported to have a chemical weapon on board. At the controls of one of the Eagles on that Memorial Day holiday was Mark "Wit" Fogel, flying off the wing of his flight leader, "Bishop." The fighters quickly gained altitude and went supersonic, accelerating past the sound barrier to intercept their target: Air France Flight 022, a wide-body Airbus A330 departing from Charles de Gaulle Airport in Paris and scheduled to land at John F. Kennedy International Airport in New York.

As AF022 flew over the Atlantic Ocean, none of its passengers were aware that Fogel and his teammate were trailing behind, with the airliner under radar and weapons lock. As Fogel told the audience from the TEDx Dayton stage in 2018, their job was to execute the president's orders to shoot it down without delay if that order came.[5] Fortunately, it never did. As Fogel and Bishop kept station at the ready behind the airliner, investigators across the law-enforcement, civil-aviation, and air-defense landscapes determined that it should be followed but allowed to land. Once on the ground, the plane was emptied and all the passengers' luggage inspected on the tarmac. The threat proved to be a hoax—as did nearly a dozen other threats to airliners across the country that day.[6]

It is amazing to think about: the US Air Force entrusts $100 million aircraft with enormous firepower in the hands of individual pilots without any hardwired controls on what happens next. "There is no one in the cockpit with me," said Fogel. "There is no system back at headquarters controlling the arming of the weapons, the decisions of the pilots, or the ability of my thumb to press a button on the control stick that would launch my missile at Air France Flight 22." But in Fogel's words, what is even more amazing is that "such trust is well placed . . . because, simply, an American fighter squadron is the most effective team on the planet."

RH: It's a big statement. When he appeared as a guest on *The Learning Leader Show*, I asked Fogel about making such an audacious claim. He explained that what makes that effectiveness attainable and such trust possible is the culture of the fighter squadron. It compels every member, regardless of rank, to abide by the mission-oriented approach to training, the improvement-oriented approach to debriefing, and the humility-oriented importance of following as much as leading.

Fighter pilots are constantly preparing for and flying two to three training sorties per week. Through the sheer force of repetition over time, they hone their skills at operating a fighter jet as a weapons platform. But, Fogel says, "The real training and learning takes place in the debrief. We spend hours poring over video, computer-graphic reenactments, radio calls, everything. We diagnose exactly what went right and what didn't and why. The debriefs can last multiple days to describe ten minutes of action."[7]

One thing that makes the culture of a fighter squadron unique is the egalitarian nature of the debrief. The person who leads the meeting and directs the feedback is not necessarily the highest-ranking officer in the room. Even though the military is the prototype of a hierarchical organization with its triangle of rank, the responsibility for running the show in the debrief lies with whoever was the flight leader of the mission. That, according to Fogel, can mean that a twentysomething captain is at the front of the room critically analyzing the performance of a general and telling that thirty-year veteran fighter pilot in front of the team, "You screwed this one up. This was bad. Let's dig in. Let's talk about this."

I asked Fogel how it would be possible for a subordinate to publicly criticize a senior leader like that. I have rarely seen a regional manager telling a VP, "You came on the sales call because we needed an executive presence, but you screwed it up. Here's how and what went wrong." Fogel pointed to the culture and what is expected versus what isn't acceptable. "That general came up in the same environment," he said. "It's just known from day one; the subculture is you check your rank at the door." The squadron briefing room is an environment of extreme trust in which the cockiness of the *Top Gun* stereotype is unacceptable. A key element to the team is that trust is built through competence and character. All members of that team have proven they have earned the right to be in the room. From the squadron's perspective, humility is the critical quality required to be part of the team because they care more about mission success and debrief fact-finding than anything else—including rank and especially ego.

LEADERS WHO FOLLOW

Being a compelling leader means leading in a way that makes it easy for others to follow. Fogel referenced the work of Amy Edmondson on how creating an environment of psychological safety is critical for the leader–follower relationship. All members of the team must feel safe speaking up when it's warranted and when feedback is given in all directions. Within the fighter squadron, pilots are trained in both how to give and receive feedback in the debrief. We tend to think of getting feedback as a skill subordinates need to learn, but Fogel's point is clear: leaders have to do it as well. They have to be able and willing to model both sides of the leader–follower dynamic. As a leader, they step into the follower role when they seek out and accept feedback from subordinates. As a follower, they step into the role of leader when they ask hard questions and provide feedback up the chain to their own superiors.

The relationship between leading and following is an interesting one. Followers are required to make any form of leadership possible. Not only that, but most of us spend more time in our lives following than we do leading. Yet the allure of leadership still beckons. Only when we step into a leadership role or assume leadership responsibilities do we fully realize the value of being a great follower. Leaders need followers, and great leaders need great followers. The more we lead, the more we understand the true dualistic aspect and impact of servant leadership. The best leaders constantly bounce between the two.

"In a fighter squadron . . . as you're flying a mission, you recognize that no matter your role in that mission, you've got facets that, in this ten-second span or this thirty-second span, I'm going to have to do something that's going to lead," Fogel explained. "And in this other thirty-second span, someone else is going to take the lead on what's happening. You are constantly code-shifting . . . We all have gaps in our knowledge. We still need to learn new things. And where you've got that gap . . . you've got to take a step back, be humble, and recognize that's not your strength. Those that know about it, give them the keys to the car, give them the power and say, 'I'm following you. I'm learning from you. You've got this. Tell me what to do. Advise me. Help me understand.'"

Coaching staffs are great examples of leaders who also follow. Though each team has a head coach, assistant coaches typically have specific areas of expertise in which they take control of players and teams. Discussions occur between the head coach and assistant coaches regarding what the head coach wants, but from there, the assistant coach becomes the leader. An excellent head coach provides confidence and support by following what the assistant coach lays out. Head coaches who attempt to micromanage all aspects of their program compromise the commitment and talents of their assistant coaches. To lead best, a head coach must be willing to follow well.

Like any other team, a coaching staff is composed of individuals who approach their role at different levels. Some ignore their role altogether. They do what they want to do, when they want to do it, with no regard for what the team needs. They always put themselves first.

Others accept their role. These coaches do what they are asked to do. They fulfill their job requirements and may or may not enjoy their position. And there are those who embrace their roles. These are the people you want on your coaching staff. They are there to serve the needs of the team in any way possible, for as long as necessary, and no job is beneath them. The team is always their priority.

Parenting is another example of following as a leader. In a parenting team, there are areas in which one parent is more proficient than the other, or where one has a different perspective than the other. It's important to be self-aware enough to recognize this in yourself and your partner so that you each truly operate within your strengths. However, as one parent leads, the other must become an unwavering follower. As we all know, if there is a crack in the consistency of the parenting wall, kids will find it and exploit it as surely as water will pass through a crack in a rock.

A healthy leader–follower culture is not created overnight. It takes time and deliberate actions to develop the competence and character needed to be a contributing member of the team. The world-class performance of fighter squadrons like Fogel's prove that this is possible. Like most great things in life, it's not easy, there are no hacks, and it takes time.

──────────────── TAKE ACTION ────────────────

Exercise: Have To/Get To

Why: To grow appreciation

How: What does "have to" imply? What does "get to" imply? What are some things you say you "have to" do? What are some things you say you "get to" do? Consider your list of have-tos. How would changing your perspective to "get to" affect the way you go about doing them?

Exercise: Ignore, Accept, Embrace

Why: To foster commitment

How: What does ignoring your role look like? What does accepting your role look like? What does embracing your role look like? Share five characteristics for each mindset about your role.

CHAPTER 16

Our Level

You don't become confident by shouting affirmations in the mirror, but by having a stack of undeniable proof that you are who you say you are. Outwork your self-doubt.

—Alex Hormozi

We Got No Game," proclaimed one headline in the *Washington Post* in the aftermath of the unthinkable.[1] Not only was a team of NBA stars not going to be winning the gold medal in the 2004 Olympics, but they would not even be playing in the gold-medal game, having lost 89–81 to Argentina in the semifinal. A team of better players got beaten by a better team. It was the third loss for the Americans over the course of their two weeks in Athens, which began with a nineteen-point drubbing from Puerto Rico in the opening game of the tournament.

After the loss, with a bronze medal still left to play for, the players of USA Basketball were in shock. "None of the US players showered after the game," recalled an Olympic staff security guard. "Dwyane Wade threw his bag ahead. Then walked to his bag and picked it up. And threw it again, all the way to the bus." Tim Duncan, the two-time NBA Most Valuable Player and co-captain of the team, "was on the pavement between two garbage cans, flat on his back. He looked like he was homeless. People had to step around him to pass."[2] With his hands covering his face, Duncan was in tears.

Kobe Bryant, one of the best players in the world at the time, was not on the 2004 team. He would be part of the team heading to the 2008 Olympics in Beijing within the framework of a revamped USA Basketball program, with the mission of not only reclaiming the gold medal but of restoring Team USA's place as the dominant force in international basketball.

In preparation, Team USA conducted a training camp in Las Vegas, enabling the players to live and practice together as a team. One night, the players headed out for a night of partying along the Las Vegas Strip. "We all go out," recalls team member Carlos Boozer. "Everybody but Kob. We dressed to impress. Got our fly stuff on. We had a good time. Come back to the hotel about five thirty or six in the morning, and guess who's in the lobby on his way to the gym?"[3]

"Kobe is downstairs in the lobby with his bag and his sneakers and his gloves, like weight-lifting gloves," Carmelo Anthony told producers of the Netflix documentary *The Redeem Team*. "Yeah, he different," noted LeBron James. "This motherfucker Kobe was already, like, drenched in sweat." Anthony looked at his watch and couldn't believe it. "Man, I'm going to sleep. I'll see you at practice." As the rest of the players rode the elevator up to their rooms, they couldn't help but take note. "This guy's really dedicated," said Boozer.

Bryant's example didn't take long to have an effect. "Next thing you know, it goes from just Kobe going at five thirty in the morning to LeBron and D-Wade. By the end of the week, the whole team was getting up every morning," Boozer recounted, "and we're on Kobe's schedule." Anthony described the impact of Bryant's example as a domino effect: "Once you start seeing the greats in there doing they thing and leading that pack, then it's like, 'Oh, I'm here. I'm with you. Let's go.'"

Bryant raised the level of his teammates' work ethic by his actions, not his words. He led by example, showing them what a standard of excellence looked like. His level of intensity raised the bar for everyone else, including an Olympic team made up of the NBA's brightest stars.

Bryant demanded more of himself than most and had been doing so since he was a young boy. As an eleven-year-old, he filled out a questionnaire given to him by his school counselor. In answer to the question "What do you want to do when you're older?" Bryant wrote, "The NBA." The answer struck the counselor as a bit far-fetched. "Kobe, that's not realistic," the counselor told him. "That's a one-in-a-million chance. Pick something more realistic."

"I will be that one," Bryant answered.[4]

STANDARDS > RULES

When we boil a demand for excellence down to its roots, we are left with a clear look at our personal standards. That's all we're really talking about. From an individual perspective, we are responsible for our personal standards. No one else gets that job, and no one else gets the blame when we fall short of them.

Standards are empowering. They are often stated in the positive, as they are expectations that allow a group to perform at maximum capacity. Rules, on the other hand, are often expressed in the negative because they are restrictive by nature.

BC: My rule used to be that if you were late to practice, you had to do a certain number of wind sprints, or if you missed practice, you had to sit out a certain number of quarters on the bench during the next game. But then, six years into coaching, I had a kid on my team who had to stay home to get his little sister on the bus, so he was late to practice. He didn't have his own car. It made me think, *That's not right. This kid who overslept has the same punishment for missing practice as this kid who has to get his sister on the bus. That doesn't make sense to me.* I realized that rules lock you into a way of doing things. So I started letting go of rules.

Standards provide built-in flexibility. If you have a standard of "Be responsible," then according to that standard, getting your little sister on the bus and then coming to practice is meeting the expectation no less than the players whose only responsibility is being dressed and ready to practice on time. You may be criticized and accused of playing favorites. It's not an easy road to navigate, for sure. But the trust and support you develop with your team while doing this is incredibly important.

Traditionally, we appreciate the clarity of rules. You either follow them or not. Either you're in trouble or you're not. Traditional leadership says, "You need clean lines of expectation. It's got to be clear and free from ambiguity so people know what to do." You don't have to have a conversation. "Both guys were late. Both get the same punishment. I'm not going to listen to why. It doesn't matter." The more nuanced approach means you have to talk to them and know what's going on. You may learn that his parent is a single mom who has to get her younger child to daycare and catch public transportation just to get to work at all. Looking beyond rules means having to wrestle with that fact.

Transformational leadership works by reinforcing standards that reflect core values, not by enforcing rules. My core values guide our standards. Is that kid being tough by staying home and getting his sister on the bus and then getting to practice as quickly as he can? Yes. Unified? Yes. Showing love? Yes. That seems very clear. The thought of upholding that standard may seem hard when someone else fails to live up to it and protests, "Hey, I was late because I overslept, but he was late too, and I got into trouble, but he didn't." It may be *harder* than blindly enforcing a rule without discretion, but it need not be hard, and it's certainly not impossible. In fact, it becomes a new positive in that it provides an opportunity for a clarifying team conversation to model and reinforce team values and standards. With regard to standards in particular, fair is not equal and equal is not fair.

When Oscar Munoz was hired as the CEO of United Airlines in 2015, he conducted a useful exercise that all of us should think about doing regularly. He gathered his senior leadership team and asked, "What are the ten dumbest rules that are currently in place, and how quickly can we eliminate them?" As the answers came flying in, Munoz and his team proceeded to tackle each of the dumb rules one by one and got rid of them.[5]

The payoff for this kind of approach takes time to realize. Excellence can come slowly. Rule implementation and enforcement is both faster and easier if the goal is accomplishing something quick and transactional. But if we are committed to being transformational, the opportunity to have these conversations is a valuable use of time rather than a waste of it.

BC: My son, Gabe, has been committed to maximizing himself as a basketball player since he was about eight years old. From a parenting perspective, I've always viewed sports as a platform to help young people learn and grow. Demanding excellence of himself is certainly a critical part of that, as I believe this mindset bleeds into all aspects of life. I clearly remember one of the first times this idea registered for my son without my prodding.

When he was eleven years old, Gabe was playing for the North Coast Blue Chips AAU basketball team at a tournament in Las Vegas. Before he went to bed the first night at the hotel, he asked me if he could shoot or work out in the morning before the team's games. At this point, working out was a regular once- or twice-a-day occurrence for Gabe. But with several potential games looming that day and no other teammates getting up in the morning to go shoot, this wasn't going to be a team thing. It was an intentional decision on his part.

After several calls to connections I had in Vegas, I found a gym about a fifteen-minute Uber ride away. We left the hotel at 6 AM and returned around 8 AM. When he got back to his room, his teammates were all still asleep. He followed the same 6 AM workout routine all four days of the tournament. I couldn't tell you how he played in those tournament games, nor does it matter, but I know he took a major step forward in demanding excellence from himself. This expectation Gabe has for himself has not faded over time. As a matter of fact, it's been reinforced. One of the simplest ways to check for commitment is to make a viable excuse available. Some mornings, due to facility conflicts, we are forced to lift weights at 6 AM rather than have our regular Breakfast Club. On those days, most would just miss their skill work. Gabe ignores the acceptable excuse to miss his workout and chooses to have his Breakfast Club at 4:45 AM and then lift weights. It's simply a choice.

Excellence depends on two things: your standards and how committed you are to upholding them. It is important to note that the true pursuit of excellence is entrenched in the process, not the outcome. Because if "winning a state championship" is the standard, then winning a state championship the night before would be reason enough to take the next morning of Breakfast Club off. But that wasn't the standard for Gabe and his teammate, Tom House. Excellence, not winning, is the standard they hold themselves to. If we are not careful, we will be fooled into thinking that winning exempts us from the very process that led us there. Even the day after winning their school's first-ever state championship, excellence was still the standard. There they were at 6 AM Breakfast Club the next morning.

STEWARD OF THE NARRATIVE

Scott Belsky is the chief product officer of Adobe, the company that invented the PDF document file format and whose Photoshop image-editing software has become a verb in the way that "Google it" means to look up information. He took over that role after Adobe acquired the company he founded, Behance, in 2012.

"Culture," says Belsky, "is just a series of stories that are repeated that people resonate with that stand for something." During his appearance on *The Learning Leader Show*, Belsky highlighted the role of narrator as something critical for leaders to embrace. He calls it being "the steward of the narrative."

"As the leader, you are also the steward of the narrative," he said on the podcast. "If you are not narrating the journey for your team, if you're not telling them the milestones you're passing, the state lines you're crossing, if you're not merchandising the progress being made, you can't expect the team to stick together long enough to figure it out . . . When day-to-day reality kicks in and you start to fall behind on life, you need to be narrated through."[6]

This is particularly true when it comes to the telling of stories that perpetuate the standards of excellence throughout a team and its culture. To coach (whether in sports or professional development) is to never tire of sharing the vision, honestly assessing where we are on the journey, and providing hope that we can achieve our goals. We steward this narrative as much with our actions as we do with our words. People need to be able to see and feel the story of our team clearly and consistently.

BC: I can close my eyes and see how I want our team to play and how I want them to act. The role of the coach, or leader, is to make this a reality. That's the art of leadership: making the narrative we have in our head tangible. We always begin with our core values. These serve as guardrails that keep us on track, preventing us from veering too far from the central theme of the narrative.

From there, we gather input from our team through our process-based team goal. That establishes a list of desired attributes of our team from which our daily actions are identified. From this point on, it's our coaches' job to consistently help our players do three things to ensure we are living our narrative.

1. **Reflect.** We need to allow them time to reflect on where we are and where we need to be. We do this through our daily debriefs following each practice and our skill sessions preceding practice.

2. **Remind.** We need to remind the team what we committed to. We accomplish this through simple and consistent communication. We say it and talk about it daily. If you are ever wondering if you're talking about it too much, let me assure you: you aren't. Say it, say it again, and then say it some more.

3. **Reinforce.** We reinforce the narrative. The narrative we work toward becomes the standard we constantly strive for. We like to think of this from a minimalistic mindset. If everything is important, then nothing is. Clarity is king. Drawn from our core values, it's the only thing we talk about.

———————————— TAKE ACTION ————————————

Exercise: Create Your Personal Standards

Why: To gain clarity on your personal standards

How: Write on a single page:

- Your purpose
- Your core values
- Your critical behaviors
- Your mantras
- Your ethos

CHAPTER 17

Advantage Us

A good father understands that inheritance is passed on in living even more than in dying. It's delivered not in a lump sum but in a daily deposit of presence and care.

—Sam Deford[1]

How we talk about things and what we say matters a lot in shaping how we think about them. Do we use objective nouns and verbs to describe the circumstances facing us, or do we use judgmental adjectives that subjectively frame things in a positive or negative light?

RH: I've noticed that the language used for weather is interesting. Whenever it's raining, most people say, "It's bad weather." I think language matters. And that language tells a child that we are reliant on externally "good" conditions to go out and have a good time. I think we should change the language. It's not "bad" weather. It's *raining*. Rain can be embraced. We can enjoy the rain. It's not good or bad. It just *is*.

My seven-year-old daughter, Charlie, had a soccer game during a big rainstorm. As we drove to the game, we talked about what's within our control and what's not, and how we can't let it dictate how we approach our days. In this case, we couldn't control the weather. We could only control how we performed in it. On that particular day, it rained a lot. Charlie played the whole game, and she loved it. Afterward, she said, "I loved playing in the rain. I hope it rains our next game, too."

Two days later, it was raining again. Charlie came and found me and said, "Daddy, it's raining. Will you jump on the trampoline with me?" As we jumped in the rain and laughed for an hour, I kept thinking, *These are the good ol' days.*

BC: Heading into the 2020–2021 basketball season, many things were up in the air. The country was coming out of lockdown due to the COVID-19 pandemic. Like everything else, it was uncertain how high-school sports were going to work. Most schools in Ohio had made it through their fall seasons in a modified fashion, as games had been canceled and seasons shortened to allow the student athletes to play safely.

Prior to the season, we had decided that we weren't going to allow the inevitable distractions to become a negative for us. We knew games were going to get canceled for various reasons beyond our control. We knew games would be quiet and lack the regular energy because only family members were allowed to attend. We knew we would have players unable to play at random times due to sickness or possible infection. Rather than waiting to make all of that an excuse, we decided to make it our advantage. Any time there was something that could be portrayed as a negative, we responded with "Advantage us."

As it turned out, the "advantage us" mentality was more powerful than we'd imagined. When we were shut down and not allowed to practice as a team multiple times during the pandemic, our guys didn't flinch. They found ways to go running, ride bikes, and do workouts regardless of the situation. Each time they chose to attack the adversity rather than use it as an excuse, the "advantage us" mentality grew. We knew others were experiencing similar challenges and discomfort, but we were confident in our ability to handle the chaos better. No matter the challenge or setback, our players embraced the "advantage us" mindset.

Eventually, we returned to the court. But rather than requiring time to reconnect and get back into the flow of things, our guys were more connected to each other and more committed to the team than they had been prior to the separation. The time apart literally *had* been turned into an advantage for us. This shared appreciation and ownership of the challenges from that year fueled our team's historic season.

The only certainty in life is that adversity will strike at some point. It's not a matter of if but when. And it's going to keep striking. We don't control that part—but we do control how we choose to respond to those tough moments. The ability of our team to respond positively to adversity is critical to maximizing our potential. As leaders, our job is to get the people we lead ready for the inevitable struggles ahead.

The most effective leaders view themselves as coaches and teachers who prepare their teams to respond to adverse situations. In today's world, we most often see adversity avoidance rather than adversity response as the standard. Our job is to make adversity response the expectation. Here are two specific actions we can take as leaders to capitalize on our competitive responses.

1. **Embrace the pack.** Life is a team sport. We are all made better when surrounded by others sharing our vision. A team unified in purpose and standards allows us to lean into our strengths and compensate for our weaknesses. Teams also infuse courage into the individual, and it's courage that allows us to respond positively when adversity stares us in the face.

2. **Focus on the process.** A fixation on results presents a formidable obstacle for confronting adversity with the proper competitive response. When we consider the moments in our lives that we are the most proud of, they are usually connected to overcoming adversity. Typically, we think it's that outcome we seek, but the fleeting nature of the accomplishment sheds light on the true aspect of fulfillment, which is the process we chose to embrace in the pursuit.

It isn't about a team achieving a performance goal by being held to a set of rules by a hierarchical team captain enforcing the traditional leadership dictates of their coach. It's about a group of teammates united in purpose, all understanding the standards the team has set for itself and holding themselves accountable for upholding them.

Bronnie Ware, an Australian caregiver, spent her life caring for patients during their last days. Her book *The Top Five Regrets of the Dying: A Life Transformed by the Dearly Departing* chronicles her conversations with patients and compiles their regrets into a list. Though the book title reflects on the dying, the contents provide a blueprint for fulfilled living.

As you read the list, consider a simple question: Does this apply to an internal scoreboard or an external one?

1. *"I wish I'd had the courage to live a life true to myself, not the life others expected of me."*
To live a life true to ourselves, we have to first know ourselves truthfully. Discovering that knowledge and then living a life in accordance with it takes courage on both fronts. First, it takes courage to truly discover who you want to be, compared to who you currently are. The reality of that distinction is not something everyone is ready to face, let alone engage with. The truth that we are not behaving like the person we think we are is a hard pill to swallow. Second, consistently choosing to engage in the behaviors necessary to become that person requires its own dose of courage. Detaching your self-image from the defining judgment of others is one of the key steps in that process. Here is this first regret expressed another way: "I wish I'd lived my life according to the core values of my internal scoreboard, not by the measurements and dictates of an external scoreboard."

2. *"I wish I'd not worked so hard."*
As Ware notes, the main concern of people expressing this regret is about how they chose to spend their time. The regret of "working so hard" wasn't about the difficulty of the work itself. They weren't wishing they had avoided challenging tasks. It was that they had

prioritized work over more important things, primarily their relationships with their family and friends. The internal scoreboard is built on our values and purpose. It is where the intangibles of life such as love, friendship, and kinship are counted. The external scoreboard centers on the socially visible markers of success. This regret, like the first, is about spending too much time living according to the wrong score.

3. *"I wish I'd had the courage to express my feelings."*
This is a different facet of the first regret: that of courage, self, and truth. This regret speaks to the inability or unwillingness to be true to our values and purpose. More pointedly, it is about a habitual reticence to share something intimate for fear it will be criticized, mocked, or rejected. But these fears are really about the opinions of those outside our foxhole. When we are worried too much about them, we will choose to appease others' feelings over faithfully giving voice to our own. A group of 3 AM friends who all have a similar commitment to the values intrinsic to our own internal scoreboard provides a safe, supportive environment for developing the courage muscle required to be honest with others about how we feel.

4. *"I wish I'd stayed in touch with my friends."*
Relationships are a key aspect of our internal scoreboards. Personal definitions of success, as opposed to society's take on it, always connect to our relationships with and impact on others. When relationships are viewed as the networking aspect of climbing the ladder, that is the external scoreboard at work. After all, it's not about what you know; it's about who you know, right? However, friends are not cogs in a networking machine. Friends bring support, fulfillment, happiness, and joy to our lives. More than anything, friendships flow in both

directions: we give and we get. We love and are loved. There's nothing about it that pertains to an external scoreboard.

5. *"I wish I'd let myself be happier."*
Where does happiness come from? It's a question with a lot of depth, but it doesn't need to be complicated. We believe happiness is the byproduct of gratitude. We can't buy it, we can't build it, and we can't work our way to it. Happiness is the result of appreciating what we have, what we do, and who we are. The moment of enjoyment we experience from a deal, championship, or blue checkmark quickly fades as we look to begin our next pursuit. But happiness is always available and never needs to fade. It is accessible daily, moment to moment. It's an internal scoreboard with an external interface.

CONCLUSION

Those in Ware's care were all keeping score throughout their lives. We all do this. It's a practice that's been ingrained in us since childhood. The score is and always will be an integral part of our lives.

The question is not "Are you keeping score?" The answer is yes. We all are.

The question is "What score are you keeping?" That is the question that matters because you *do* get to choose. Contrary to what societal norms imply, *you* control how you define success. You get to decide what you value and what you don't. You determine the perspective you take on each success and failure. While none of these decisions has the power to dictate a final outcome, they do significantly impact something far more important: the process you choose to follow.

It's the process that you need to master, not the outcome. A scoreboard that measures the *how* of a process rather than the *what* of an outcome is the scoreboard that matters most. Unfortunately, it's a scoreboard we rarely check until devastation and humiliation rear their ugly heads. Oddly enough, rock bottom often bestows the gifts of clarity of purpose and directness of process. Failure becomes the hand that directs our focus inward.

Thankfully, you don't have to wait for despair to prompt you to become intentional. You can choose to shift your mind and heart to the score that matters right now. It's not a complicated process: discover your purpose, identify your values, create your critical behaviors, and live them faithfully every day in all aspects of your life.

Of course, simple does not mean easy. We acknowledge that being both intentional about and faithful to this is the challenge. It is hard. As a matter of fact, we are thankful it's not easy. The opportunity to impact lives *should* come with a hefty price tag. This cost often takes the form of your comfort.

The payoff is waiting.

Excellence is possible.

Impact is achievable.

It's time to make the choice to intentionally live the fulfilling life you were meant to live.

It's time to focus on *the score that matters*.

Acknowledgments

RYAN HAWK

Brook: Thank you for pushing me toward excellence, living your values, and writing this book with me. Tyler Cowen told me to never pass up an opportunity to partner with someone who is world-class at what they do. That's you. Thank you.

Geron, Sherri, BC, Eli: Our squad. It's only the beginning. Thank you for making me better every day.

Matt Holt and the BenBella team: Thank you for taking over and making this book much better than it was when you got it. Looking forward to working together a lot more in the future.

Casey Ebro, Liam Murray, Jeff Estill, Lance Salyers, Dan Smith, and Mary Beth Conlee: Your thoughtful feedback has made this book much better. Thank you.

Learning Leader Circle Members: Thank you for being part of my inner circle. I cherish our time together. Your belief in the Learning Leader mission from day one means the world to me.

Sam Kaufman and Bert Bean: I'm inspired by how much you love and care for the people you serve. Thank you for believing in me and providing the opportunity to partner with Insight Global moving forward. I've loved our past two and a half years together and look forward to many more.

Listeners of *The Learning Leader Show*: Your feedback is the juice! Thank you for your continued support and willingness to share your personal stories about how my podcast has helped you. It means more than you realize. And . . . if you're part of the "End of the Podcast Club," send me a note: Ryan@LearningLeader.com.

My family: Mom, Pistol, Berk, Beth, AJ, and Laura, thank you for always having my back and believing in me.

Brooklyn, Ella, Addison, Payton, and Charlie: I am so proud of you. I love you very much.

Miranda, thank you for your unconditional love. Thank you for making every situation better. I love your work ethic, grit, toughness, and beauty. I am so grateful we get to do life together.

BROOK CUPPS

Thank you, tough—for ignoring excuses.

Thank you, passionate—for providing the extra.

Thank you, unified—for lifting me to my potential.

Thank you, thankful—for helping me accept and embrace.

Thank you, excellence—for never arriving.

Thank you, courage—for not knowing and going for it anyway.

Thank you, dirt—for keeping me, me.

Thank you, less—for always being more.

Thank you, foxhole friends—for being the only kind.

Thank you, Mom—for being a fighter.

Thank you, Dad—for being the strongest person I'll ever know.

Thank you, Bets—for your smile; it lights my world and makes our family go.

Thank you, Dink—for your love of life and all things in it.

Thank you, Bud—for your ball and your devoted pursuit of your dreams.

Thank you, God—for putting me here, with these people, with this calling . . . and forgiving me.

Notes

LET'S GOOOOO!

1. "Address by Andrew Carnegie at the Unveiling of a Statue to Burns," ElectricScotland.com, accessed July 24, 2023, https://electricscotland.com/burns/carnegie.htm.
2. Ibid.
3. Andrew Carnegie, *The Autobiography of Andrew Carnegie* (New Delhi: General Press, 2022, Kindle Edition).
4. Jack Raines, "Infinite Games," *Young Money* (blog), March 3, 2023, https://www.youngmoney.co/p/infinite-games.

CHAPTER 1

1. Lewis Carroll, *Alice's Adventures in Wonderland* (Chicago: W.B. Conkey, 1920).
2. Tasha Eurich, "Episode #204: Dr. Tasha Eurich—How to Become More Self-Aware," May 14, 2017, in *The Learning Leader Show*, podcast, 44:55, https://learningleader.com/tashaeurich/.

3. Cody Keenan, "Episode #499: Cody Keenan—Working with the Most Powerful Person in the World, Taking Big Risks & the Art of Speechwriting," November 13, 2022, in *The Learning Leader Show*, podcast, 54:40, https://learningleader.com/codykeenan499/.

4. Kori Schulman, "Chief Speechwriter Cody Keenan's Commencement Address to NYU's Wagner School of Public Service," ObamaWhite House.archives.gov, May 26, 2015, accessed July 25, 2023, https://obamawhitehouse.archives.gov/blog/2016/08/18/chief-speechwriter-cody-keenans-commencement-address-nyus-wagner-school-public.

5. Jay Shetty, *Think Like a Monk* (New York: Simon & Schuster, 2020).

CHAPTER 2

1. Steven Pressfield, *The War of Art: Break Through the Blocks and Win Your Inner Creative Battles* (New York: Black Irish Books, 2002), 12.

2. "This pre-game speech from Mike Bianco is legendary! 'Once your commitment is greater than your feelings, that's when you get results!'" Ultimate Baseball Training, August 14, 2021, Facebook video, https://www.facebook.com/UltimateBaseballTraining/videos/this-pre-game-speech-from-mike-bianco-is-legendary-once-your-commitment-is-great/541336743846808/.

3. Michael Easter, "Episode #465: Michael Easter—Embrace Discomfort to Reclaim Your Wild, Healthy, Happy Self (The Comfort Crisis)," March 27, 2022, in *The Learning Leader Show*, podcast, 1:05:33, https://learningleader.com/michaeleaster/.

CHAPTER 3

1. "Reentry Vehicles: Spheres vs. Blunt Bodies," NASA, accessed July 31, 2023, https://www.hq.nasa.gov/pao/History/SP-4209/ch3-4.htm.

2. "Vostok and Mercury: First Flights into Space," NASA, accessed July 31, 2023, https://www.hq.nasa.gov/pao/History/SP-4209/ch3-5.htm.

3. Jeff Shesol, "Episode #504: Jeff Shesol—Moonshot Goals, Driver vs. Passenger Mentality & Creating Your Own Fate," December 18, 2022, in

The Learning Leader Show, podcast, 59:55, https://learningleader.com/jeffshesol504/.

4. Donald Miller, "Episode #496: Donald Miller—Be the Hero, Add Value to Others & Don't Trust Fate to Write Your Story (LIVE! In Nashville)," October 23, 2022, in *The Learning Leader Show*, podcast, 50:09, https://learningleader.com/donaldmiller496/.

5. Ben Cohen, "The Power of Ohio State's Positive Thinking," *Wall Street Journal*, January 8, 2015, https://www.wsj.com/articles/the-power-of-ohio-states-positive-thinking-1420738209.

6. Tim Kight, "Episode #074: Tim Kight—The Secret Weapon Behind Ohio State's Success," November 23, 2015, in *The Learning Leader Show*, podcast, 52:24, https://learningleader.com/episode-074-tim-kight-the-secret-weapon-behind-ohio-states-success/.

7. Ty Schalter, "Embarrassing MNF Blowout Loss to Chiefs Sounds Death Knell for Patriots Dynasty," Bleacher Report, September 30, 2014, https://bleacherreport.com/articles/2215366-embarrassing-mnf-blowout-loss-to-chiefs-sounds-death-knell-for-patriots-dynasty.

8. Eric Wilbur, "Something Is Seriously Wrong with the Patriots, and Whatever It Is Won't Be a Quick Fix," Boston.com, September 30, 2014, https://www.boston.com/sports/new-england-patriots/2014/09/30/something_is_seriously_wrong_with_the_patriots_and/.

9. "Bill Belichick Press Conference Transcript: 'We're on to Cincinnati,'" New England Patriots, October 1, 2014, https://www.patriots.com/news/bill-belichick-press-conference-transcript-we-re-on-to-cincinnati-208851.

10. Henry McKenna, "5 Funniest Moments from Bill Belichick's Spring Press Conferences," Patriots Wire, June 17, 2017, https://patriotswire.usatoday.com/2017/06/17/5-funniest-moments-from-bill-belichicks-spring-press-conferences/.

11. Ryan Holiday, "Episode #485: Ryan Holiday—The Power of Self Control, Loving the Process & Building Endurance (Discipline Is Destiny)," August 13, 2022, in *The Learning Leader Show*, podcast, 1:07:04, https://learningleader.com/ryanholiday485/.

12. "It's All Quality Time," Daily Dad, accessed July 31, 2023, https://dailydad.com/its-all-quality-time/.

CHAPTER 5

1. Tim Urban (@waitbutwhy), Twitter, February 13, 2022, 2:20 PM, https://twitter.com/waitbutwhy/status/1492941874889375746?lang=en.
2. Jocko Willink, "Episode #234: Jocko Willink—Why Discipline Equals Freedom, December 3, 2017, in *The Learning Leader Show*, podcast, 55:30, https://learningleader.com/episode-234-jocko-willink-discipline-equals-freedom.
3. David McCullough, *The Wright Brothers* (New York: Simon & Schuster, 2015).
4. Eric Adams, "Episode #494: Mayor Eric Adams—Authenticity, Honesty & Changing from Within . . . A Conversation with the Mayor of New York City," October 9, 2022, in *The Learning Leader Show*, podcast, 33:41, https://learningleader.com/ericadams494.

CHAPTER 6

1. Jim Collins, "Episode #216: Jim Collins—How to Go from Good to Great," July 30, 2017, in *The Learning Leader Show*, podcast, 1:10:02, https://learningleader.com/episode-216-jim-collins-go-good-great/.
2. Todd Henry, "Episode #489: Todd Henry—Asking Uncomfortable Questions, Solving Big Problems & Casting Your Vision," September 11, 2022, in *The Learning Leader Show*, podcast, 1:11:40, https://learningleader.com/toddhenry489/.
3. Adam Grant, "Are You a Giver or a Taker? | Adam Grant," TED, January 24, 2017, YouTube video, 13:28, https://youtu.be/YyXRYgjQXX0.
4. Jimmy Donaldson, "How Mr. Beast Became Successful on YouTube," PowerfulJRE, March 7, 2022, YouTube video, 14:56, https://youtu.be/3A8kawxMOcQ.
5. Luke Burgis, "Luke Burgis—Why We Want What We Want | *The Learning Leader Show* with Ryan Hawk," Ryan Hawk, June 3, 2021, YouTube video, 56:59, https://youtu.be/LwnaVBxeN64.

6. Morgan Housel, "Episode #382: Morgan Housel—Timeless Lessons on Wealth, Greed & Happiness," September 6, 2020 in *The Learning Leader Show*, podcast, 1:02:08, https://learningleader.com/houselhawk382.

7. Jere Longman, "OLYMPICS; A Long Triumphs in the Olympic Trials," *New York Times*, February 27, 2000, https://www.nytimes.com/2000/02/27/sports/olympics-a-long-triumphs-in-the-olympic-trials.html.

8. Lindsay Crouse, "How the 'Shalane Flanagan Effect' Works," *New York Times*, November 11, 2017, https://www.nytimes.com/2017/11/11/opinion/sunday/shalane-flanagan-marathon-running.html.

9. Shalane Flanagan bio page, Team USA, accessed August 7, 2023, https://www.teamusa.com/profiles/shalane-flanagan-805529.

10. Crouse, "How the 'Shalane Flanagan Effect' Works."

11. Ibid.

12. Ibid.

CHAPTER 7

1. "Focus," Merriam-Webster.com Dictionary, Merriam-Webster, accessed August 7, 2023, https://www.merriam-webster.com/dictionary/focus.

2. Brandon Griggs, "10 Great Quotes from Steve Jobs," CNN, January 4, 2016, https://edition.cnn.com/2012/10/04/tech/innovation/steve-jobs-quotes/index.html.

3. Ryan Holiday, "Episode #485."

4. Greg McKeown, "Episode #416: Greg McKeown—How to Make It Easier to Do What Matters Most," April 25, 2021, in *The Learning Leader Show*, podcast, 1:06:00, https://learningleader.com/gregmckeown416/.

CHAPTER 8

1. "Ethos," Oxford Languages definition, accessed online September 7, 2023.

2. Rudyard Kipling, "The Law of the Jungle," Kipling Society, accessed August 7, 2023, https://www.kiplingsociety.co.uk/poem/poems_lawofjungle.htm.

3. Theodore Roosevelt, "The Man in the Arena," Theodore Roosevelt Center at Dickinson State University, accessed August 7, 2023, https://www.theodorerooseveltcenter.org/Learn-About-TR/TR-Encyclopedia/Culture-and-Society/Man-in-the-Arena.aspx.

4. "Bird IQ Test Takes Flight," Natural Sciences and Engineering Research Council, EurekAlert!, February 21, 2006, https://www.eurekalert.org/news-releases/654380.

5. Paul Rincon, "Crows and Jays Top Bird IQ Scale," Science & Environment, BBC News, last updated February 22, 2005, http://news.bbc.co.uk/2/hi/science/nature/4286965.stm.

6. Zach Dirlam, "Michigan vs. Ohio State 1969: The Game That Changed a Rivalry Forever," Bleacher Report, May 15, 2013, https://bleacherreport.com/articles/1638930-michigan-vs-ohio-state-1969-the-game-that-changed-a-rivalry-forever.

7. "The Ten Year War," Bentley Historical Library, Regents of the University of Michigan, last modified July 2005, accessed August 9, 2023, https://bentley.umich.edu/athdept/football/umosu/woodyvbo.htm.

CHAPTER 9

1. Daniel F. Chambliss, "The Mundanity of Excellence: An Ethnographic Report on Stratification and Olympic Swimmers," *Sociological Theory* 7, no. 1 (Spring 1989): https://academics.hamilton.edu/documents/themundanityofexcellence.pdf.

2. Bill Walsh, *The Score Takes Care of Itself* (New York: Portfolio, 2009), 2, Kindle.

3. Christine Hauser, "A Precinct's Hard Road Back," *New York Times*, February 24, 2008, https://www.nytimes.com/2008/02/24/nyregion/24precinct.html.

4. Eric Adams, "We Must Stop Police Abuse of Black Men," *New York Times*, December 4, 2014, https://www.nytimes.com/2014/12/05/opinion/we-must-stop-police-abuse-of-black-men.html.

5. Eric Adams, "Episode #494," *The Learning Leader Show.*

6. Kara Lawson, "Kara Lawson: Handle Hard Better," Duke Women's Basketball, July 5, 2022, YouTube video, 2:49, https://youtu.be/oDzfZOfNki4.

CHAPTER 10

1. Tre'Vaugn Howard, "After Upset Win over Germany in World Cup, Japanese Players Leave Dressing Room 'Spotless,'" CBS News, November 25, 2022, https://www.cbsnews.com/news/japan-upset-win-over-germany-japanese-players-leave-dressing-room-spotless/.
2. Cindy Boren, "Japan's World Cup Legacy Includes a Spotless Locker Room and a Thank-You Note," *Washington Post*, July 3, 2018, https://www.washingtonpost.com/news/soccer-insider/wp/2018/07/03/japans-world-cup-legacy-includes-a-spotless-locker-room-and-a-thank-you-note/.
3. Tom Brady, "Tom Brady on What's Next After Giving 32 Years to Football, Talks Future as FOX Analyst | THE HERD," The Herd with Colin Cowherd, February 6, 2023, YouTube video, 12:40, https://youtu.be/SL7ArJeU6so.
4. "Farmer | Ram Trucks," Ram Trucks, February 3, 2013, YouTube video, 2:02, https://youtu.be/AMpZ0TGjbWE.

CHAPTER 11

1. Morgan Housel, "Some Things I Think," *Collaborative Fund* (blog), April 26, 2023, https://collabfund.com/blog/thoughts/.
2. Becky Burleigh, "Becky Burleigh | The Green Dot," What Drives Winning, February 7, 2016, YouTube video, 6:27, https://youtu.be/aD1MyaAlX4o.
3. "Brett Ledbetter & Becky Burleigh—What Drives Winning (Focus on the Process)," Ryan Hawk, January 20, 2023, YouTube video, 53:23, https://youtu.be/NvhmMlJiGG0.
4. "Florida vs. Stanford (Nov 28, 2014)," NCAA, accessed August 12, 2023, http://fs.ncaa.org/Docs/stats/w_soccer_champs_records/2014/d1/html/ncaa4.htm.

5. Brett Ledbetter, *What Drives Winning* (2015), PDF excerpt, accessed August 12, 2023, https://whatdriveswinning.com/wp-content/uploads /2018/03/WDW_book-courageous-excerpt.pdf.

6. Gary Chapman, *The Five Love Languages: How to Express Heartfelt Commitment to Your Mate* (Chicago: Northfield Publishing, 1992), 140.

7. Ibid., 61.

8. Julia Boorstin, "Episode #495: Julia Boorstin—Interviewing Powerful CEOs, Building Confidence & Becoming a Talent Magnet (When Women Lead)," October 16, 2022, in *the Learning Leader Show*, podcast, 54:14, https://learningleader.com/juliaboorstin/.

9. Karen Young, "The Science of Gratitude—How It Changes People, Relationships (and Brains!) and How to Make It Work for You," Hey Sigmund, accessed August 14, 2023, https://www.heysigmund.com/the -science-of-gratitude/.

10. Eric Lindberg, "Practicing Gratitude Can Have Profound Health Benefits, USC Experts Say," USC News, November 25, 2019, https://news.usc .edu/163123/gratitude-health-research-thanksgiving-usc-experts/.

11. Cassie Holmes, "Episode #488: Cassie Holmes—How to Expand Your Time, Focus on What Matters Most & Live a Happier Life," September 4, 2022, in *The Learning Leader Show*, podcast, 52:05, https://learningleader .com/cassieholmes488/.

12. Tim Urban, "The Tail End," *Wait But Why* (blog), December 11, 2015, https://waitbutwhy.com/2015/12/the-tail-end.html.

13. "Ruavieja Commercial 2018 (English subs): #WeHaveToSeeMoreOf EachOther," Ruavieja, November 20, 2018, YouTube video, 4:25, https:// youtu.be/kma1bPDR-rE.

14. Charles T. Munger, *Poor Charlie's Almanack: The Wit and Wisdom of Charles T. Munger*, ed. Peter D. Kaufman (Marceline, MO: Donning Company, 2005).

CHAPTER 12

1. James Clear, "Why Trying to Be Perfect Won't Help You Achieve Your Goals (and What Will)," *James Clear* (blog), accessed August 14, 2023, https://jamesclear.com/repetitions.

2. McCullough, *The Wright Brothers*, 68.

3. Anita Elberse, "Number One in Formula One," *Harvard Business Review*, November–December 2022, https://hbr.org/2022/11/number-one-in-formula-one.

4. Ibid.

5. Sam Knight, "Toto Wolff, the Compulsive Perfectionist Behind Mercedes's Formula 1 Team," *New Yorker*, October 23, 2022, https://www.newyorker.com/magazine/2022/10/31/toto-wolff-the-compulsive-perfectionist-behind-mercedes-formula-1-team.

6. Elberse, "Number One in Formula One."

7. Knight, "Toto Wolff."

8. Ibid.

9. JJ Redick, "JJ Redick," January 17, 2023, in *Knuckleheads with Quentin Richardson & Darius Miles*, podcast, 1:19:06, https://omny.fm/shows/knuckleheads-with-quentin-richardson-darius-miles/jjredick.

10. Lisa D. Ordóñez, Maurice E. Schweitzer, Adam D. Galinsky, and Max H. Bazerman, "Goals Gone Wild: The Systematic Side Effects of Over-Prescribing Goal Setting," Harvard Business School, 2009, online PDF, https://www.hbs.edu/ris/Publication%20Files/09-083.pdf.

CHAPTER 13

1. Stanley McChrystal, "Episode #357: Stanley McChrystal—Leadership in Uncertain Times," March 22, 2020, in *The Learning Leader Show*, podcast, 1:13:10, https://learningleader.com/mcchrystalhawk357/.

2. Warren Buffett, "Berkshire's Corporate Performance vs. the S&P 500," February 27, 2004, online PDF, https://www.berkshirehathaway.com/letters/2003ltr.pdf.

3. Stephen Covey, "Episode #358: Stephen Covey—The One Thing That Changes Everything (Trust)," March 29, 2020, in *The Learning Leader Show*, podcast, 1:11:37, https://learningleader.com/coveyhawk358/.

4. Paul Zak, "The Neuroscience of Trust," *Harvard Business Review*, January–February 2017, https://hbr.org/2017/01/the-neuroscience-of-trust.

5. Brené Brown, *Rising Strong: The Reckoning. The Rumble. The Revolution* (New York: Spiegel & Grau, 2015), 4.

6. Liz Mineo, "Good Genes Are Nice, but Joy Is Better," *Harvard Gazette*, April 11, 2017, https://news.harvard.edu/gazette/story/2017/04 /over-nearly-80-years-harvard-study-has-been-showing-how-to-live -a-healthy-and-happy-life/.

7. Polina Pompliano, "Episode #464: Polina Pompliano—Profiles of the World's Greatest Performers, Makers vs. Managers & Building Trust Through Consistency," March 20, 2022, in *The Learning Leader Show*, podcast, 1:14:12, https://learningleader.com/polina/.

8. Andrew Brandt, "Episode #120: Andrew Brandt—Learning from a World Class Negotiator," May 1, 2016, in *The Learning Leader Show*, podcast, 49:16, https://learningleader.com/episode-120-andrew-brandt -learning-from-a-world-class-negotiator/.

CHAPTER 14

1. Jimmy Butler, "'I don't call them role players, I call them teammates' - Jimmy Butler Talks After Game 7," NBA, May 29, 2023, YouTube video, 4:43, https://www.youtube.com/watch?v=vSRwLi35DpI.

2. Peter Wohlleben, *The Hidden Life of Trees* (Vancouver: Greystone Books, 2016), 4.

3. L. David Mech, "Alpha status, dominance, and division of labor in wolf packs," *USGS Northern Prairie Wildlife Research Center* (1999): 1197–98, https://digitalcommons.unl.edu/cgi/viewcontent.cgi?article=1343& context=usgsnpwrc.

4. Ibid., 1196.

5. Ibid., 1198.

6. Virginia Morell, "Wolves Cooperate but Dogs Submit, Study Suggests," Science.org, August 19, 2014, https://www.science.org/content/article /wolves-cooperate-dogs-submit-study-suggests.

7. Ibid.

8. Kanye West, "Clique x Kanye West," Clique TV, March 12, 2015, You-Tube video, https://www.youtube.com/watch?app=desktop&v=QDdOi -gBYfg.

9. Kat Cole, "Episode #476: Kat Cole—Pragmatic Optimism, Reflection Questions, Humble Confidence, Building Trust & the Hot Shot Rule," June 12, 2022, in *The Learning Leader Show*, podcast, 1:15:23, https://learningleader.com/katcole476/.

10. Claire Meyer, "McChrystal: Focus on Empowering Frontline Decision-Makers," Asis International, September 24, 2020, https://www.asisonline.org/security-management-magazine/articles/2020/gsx-show-daily-2020/McChrystal-focus-on-Empowering-Frontline-Decision-Makers/.

11. McChrystal, "Episode #357."

CHAPTER 15

1. Ryan Hawk, *Welcome to Management* (New York: McGray-Hill, 2020), 9, Kindle.

2. Paul Smith, "Episode #501: Paul Smith—How to Tell Stories That Inspire Change and Produce Results," November 27, 2022, in *The Learning Leader Show*, podcast, 57:35, https://learningleader.com/paulsmith/.

3. Katie Nodjimbadem, "The Trashy Beginnings of 'Don't Mess with Texas,'" *Smithsonian Magazine*, March 10, 2017, https://www.smithsonianmag.com/history/trashy-beginnings-dont-mess-texas-180962490/.

4. "Stevie Ray Vaughn," March 15, 2022, Dont mess with Texas®—Official, YouTube video, 0:29, https://youtu.be/BVyZ6d_G3js.

5. Mark Fogel, "The Culture of a Fighter Squadron," TED, October 2018, https://www.ted.com/talks/mark_fogel_the_culture_of_a_fighter_squadron.

6. Meghan Keneally and Josh Margolin, "Fighter Jets Scramble Following at Least 6 Reports of Threats to Passenger Planes, Officials Say," ABC News, May 25, 2015, https://abcnews.go.com/International/fighter-jets-scramble-escort-air-france-flight-threat/story?id=31289047.

7. Mark Fogel, "Episode #513: Mark Fogel—Becoming a Great Follower, Running World-Class Debriefs, Building a Healthy Culture & Why Fighter Squadrons Are the Best Teams on Earth," February 18, 2023, in *The Learning Leader Show*, podcast, 55:45, https://learningleader.com/markfogel/.

CHAPTER 16

1. Mike Wise, "We Got No Game," *Washington Post*, August 28, 2004, https://www.washingtonpost.com/archive/politics/2004/08/28/we-got -no-game/8b706c70-b8f8-4132-a553-5064395f3a9c/.

2. Nate Penn, "Dunk'd: An Oral History of the 2004 Dream Team," July 27, 2012, GQ.com, https://www.gq.com/story/2004-olympic-basketball -dream-team.

3. Jon Weinbach, dir., *The Redeem Team*, Netflix, 2022, https://www .netflix.com/title/81452996.

4. Roland Lazenby, *Showboat: The Life of Kobe Bryant* (Boston: Little, Brown and Company, 2017).

5. Oscar Munoz, "Episode #524: Oscar Munoz (Former CEO of United Airlines)—Listening to Your Employees, Responding from Tragedy, Swinging Easy & Turning Around a Failing Company," April 29, 2023, in *The Learning Leader Show*, podcast, 1:04:47, https://learningleader .com/oscarmunoz524/.

6. Scott Belsky, "Episode #276: Scott Belsky—How to Find Your Way Through the Hardest Part of Any Venture (the Messy Middle)," September 22, 2018, in *The Learning Leader Show*, podcast, 51:55, https:// learningleader.com/scottbelskyryanhawk276/.

CHAPTER 17

1. Sam Deford, "Sonship," *Kinsmen Journal*, accessed August 14, 2023, https://www.kinsmenjournal.com/essays/sonship.

Index

About the Authors

For the past decade, **Ryan Hawk** has interviewed over six hundred of the world's most influential leaders: Jim Collins, Simon Sinek, Adam Grant, James Clear, Ryan Holiday, Kat Cole, Alex Hormozi, John Maxwell, Jocko Willink, Susan Cain, Ramit Sethi, Pat McAfee, Kirk Herbstreit, JJ Redick, Coach John Calipari, Admiral William McRaven, Liz Wiseman, George Raveling, Tom Peters, Daniel Pink, Patrick Lencioni, John Mackey, Robert Greene, General Stanley McChrystal, Seth Godin—the list goes on. *The Learning Leader Show* has been named an Apple Podcasts bestseller for the past four years and regularly ranks as one the 100 Top Business Podcasts in the world. It has millions of downloads per year. Now, as a best-selling author, keynote speaker, and world-renowned interviewer, Ryan travels the globe teaching the world's largest companies, universities, and associations about personal excellence, leadership, storytelling, sales, teamwork, and more. When Ryan speaks, you're listening to everyone he's ever interviewed. And he's interviewed more than one hundred *New York Times* best-selling authors in addition to Special Forces operators, Fortune 500 CEOs, entrepreneurs, professional athletes, and front office executives. In addition to *The Score That*

Matters, Ryan has published two other books: *Welcome to Management: How to Grow from Top Performer to Excellent Leader* (named the "best leadership book of 2020" by *Forbes*) and *The Pursuit of Excellence: The Uncommon Behaviors of the World's Most Productive Achievers* (named in *Forbes* as the "most dynamic leadership book of 2022 delivering a master-class on how to apply the most useful habits to real-life").

Brook Cupps is a teacher and head boys' basketball coach at Centerville High School in Ohio. In his twenty-fourth year in education, Brook has been a head coach for twenty-three years and is in his twelfth season at Centerville. In the classroom, he leads students in two leadership classes for which he wrote the curriculum. On the court, Brook guided Centerville to three consecutive Final Four appearances, resulting in a state championship in 2021. Between the 2021 and 2022 seasons, Centerville won a remarkable forty-five consecutive games. Prior to Centerville, Brook spent nine years as the head coach at his alma mater, St. Paris Graham High School.

In addition, Brook spent five summers assisting with the North Coast Blue Chips, where his son teamed up with Bronny James. The Chips were a national sensation in the grassroots basketball world from 2014 to 2019, winning two youth national championships. Brook also released a book, *Surrender the Outcome*, in the fall of 2021. The book is a leadership fable that loosely chronicles the progression of Brook's coaching and leadership philosophy. In addition, he publishes a weekly blog post discussing various leadership and coaching topics. Brook resides in Centerville, Ohio, with his wife, Betsy. Their daughter, Ally (22), lives in Celina, Ohio, while working at MVP Dairy, and their son, Gabe (19), is a freshman at Indiana University, where he is a member of the basketball team.